OUR READERS RAVE

Some books print fancy reviews written by fancy book critics. Borrring! At the BRI, we care more about what our faithful readers have to say.

"Since sharing my *Bathroom Reader* with my friends at school my popularity has dramatically increased. Thanks!"
—**Chance G., age 13**

"I think your *Kids Reader* is stupendous, tremendous, terrific, and splenderiffic! I can't put it down. I can't believe how much I've learned. It is one of the best books I've ever read!!!!!!!!"
—**Allison D., age 11**

"On a scale of 1 to 10, I love ur books at about a…13.5."
—**Zolly C., age 14**

"I got the Kids edition for Christmas! I love it. I frequently find myself in a position where my brother is banging on the door screaming at me to get out of the bathroom…tee hee thanks! :)"
—**Lindsay P., age 12**

"When I discovered the *Bathroom Reader For Kids Only* at the airport it changed my life. I would like to thank you…I'll never be bored again!!!!"
—**Dominika D., age 11**

"The minute I opened up the *Bathroom Reader for Kids Only*, I couldn't close it! I take it to school and all my friends want to read it! Thanks B.R.I."
—*Toria Z., age 9*

"I just wanted to shout out that you are totally awesome. My mom bought me *For Kids Only*. You're the best for making a book that just us kids can read."
—*Elyssa A., age 10*

"I really love your *Bathroom Reader*, I read it everywhere. It's better than *Harry Potter* and definitely the best thing since sliced bread."
—*Richard L., age 12*

"I have 14 year old twin boys…one reads everything, anything, and everything. The other won't read anything at all…except the *Bathroom Readers*."
—*Jonna W.*

"My daughter, Mandy, loves your first *Kids Reader*. Now she can stop stealing my books and read her own. (By the way, *Bathroom Readers* are great for ANY room of the house.)"
—*Michael F.*

"Just finished reading *For Kids Only*. (OK, I'm a 50-year-old kid but my wife and mom said it was OK.)"
—*Chris P.*

Uncle John's
ELECTRIFYING
BATHROOM READER
FOR
KIDS ONLY

By the
Bathroom Readers' Institute

Bathroom Readers' Press
Ashland, Oregon

UNCLE JOHN'S ELECTRIFYING BATHROOM READER® FOR KIDS ONLY

For information, write:
Bathroom Readers' Institute
P.O. Box 1117, Ashland, OR 97520
www.bathroomreader.com

Cover design by Michael Brunsfeld,
San Rafael, CA (*brunsfeldo@attbi.com*)

Illustrations by
Lorraine Bodger

Uncle John's Electrifying

Bathroom Reader For Kids Only

by The Bathroom Readers' Institute
ISBN: 1-59223-021-0
Library of Congress Control Number: 2003105619

Printed in the United States of America

First printing 2003

10 9 8 7 6 5 4 3 2

THANK YOU!

The Bathroom Readers' Institute thanks those people whose help has made this book possible.

Allen Orso
Jahnna Beacham
Jeff Altemus
Julia Papps
Thom Little
Lori Larson
Lorraine Therring
Brianna Bergman
George Ene Lidell
Janet Nelson
Paul Stanley, Banta Books
Bill Haduch
Wilderness Charter School
Gideon and Sam
Maggie McLaughlin
Bryan Henry
Angela Kern
Michael Brunsfeld
Scarab Media
Malcolm Hillgartner

Gordon Javna
Jay Newman
John Dollison
Jennifer & Gracie
Rick Rebhun
Mustard Press
Dee Edwards
Lorraine Bodger
Sharilyn Hovind
Kristin Marley
Bernadette Baillie
JoAnn Padgett
Mike Nicita
John Javna
Dylan Drake
Don Thomas
Maggie Javna
Catie Pratt
Porter the Wonder Dog
Thomas Crapper

When we think of amazing kids, one very special one comes to mind. Our friend Marley Pratt is eighteen years old and has been battling cancer for three years. Yet through it all, Marley never fails to inspire us with his smiling face and winning attitude. He's the toughest cowboy we know. We dedicate this book is to him.

TABLE OF CONTENTS

Because the BRI understands your reading needs, we've divided the contents by length as well as subject:
Short—A quick read
Medium—2 pages
Long—3 to 5 pages (that's not too long, is it?)

TIME MACHINE: THE FUTURE

TOYS AND GAMES

JUST FOR FUN

QUIZ ANSWERS

RESOURCE GUIDE

*   *   *

SOME THINGS NEVER CHANGE

"Children today are tyrants. They contradict their parents, gobble their food, and tyrannize their teachers."

—Socrates (469–399 B.C.)

GREETINGS FROM UNCLE JOHN

Hiya Kids,

We're back with our second book for kids, *Uncle John's ELECTRIFYING Bathroom Reader for Kids Only*. I didn't believe we could top our last effort, but you know—I think we actually did.

So, here I am on a Sunday afternoon, finally putting the finishing touches on the book so it can go off to the printer tomorrow and I realize nothing's changed since I was a kid—I'm still doing my homework at the last minute on a Sunday night! (I hope I get an A.)

First, a few announcements:

• Thanks to the thousands of kids who let us know how much they loved our last book, *Uncle John's Bathroom Reader for Kids Only*. We hope you like number two as much as you liked number one.

• Special thanks to the great Bathroom Reader staff, especially to Jahnna Beecham, our head writer supreme.

Okay. Now here's a bit of what's in this book:

• Amazing kids, like 12-year-old Craig Kielburger, who started Kids Can Free the Children, an organization that helps young people around the world. You'll also find stories of kid authors, kid inventors, and kid geniuses.

- Origins of everyday things—stuff you'll find around the house, like mirrors, towels, and toothbrushes.

- Spooky stories, like the tale of the sailing ship, *Mary Celeste*, whose entire crew vanished without a trace and remains a mystery to this day. Woo-oo-oo-o-o-o.

- And while we're on mysteries, you won't want to miss our article on the Bermuda Triangle, where dozens of planes and ships have disappeared into thin air.

- We've got some stories of animal heroes, like Roy, the dog that rescued a baby from a building ledge. And Priscilla, the pig that rescued a drowning kid.

- How about gross stuff? Spitting camels, farting snakes, stinky flowers, and a recipe for making fake boogers.

- What else? Riddles, brainteasers, movie bloopers, space facts, real-life X-men, the origin of pizza, secret languages, myths, dumb crooks, and much more.

There's something for everybody, so let's get started!

From all of us at the Bathroom Readers' Institute, including my trusted assistant, J. Porter Newman, and my talking dog, Elbow Room, remember:

When in doubt…

Go with the Flow!

—Uncle John and the BRI staff

P.S. Visit us on the Web at: *www.bathroomreader.com*

NAME THAT TOWN

Some town names describe the land around them: Grand Rapids, Twin Falls. Others celebrate famous people: Washington, Lincoln, Victoria. And others... what were the founders thinking?

- Burnt Corn, Alabama
- Twodot, Montana
- Toad Suck, Arkansas
- Worms, Nebraska
- Sucker Flat, California
- Lizard Lick, N. Carolina
- Yellow Water, Florida
- Frog Jump, Tennessee
- Snapfinger, Georgia
- Kickapoo, Illinois
- Gas, Kansas
- Boring, Oregon
- Grasshopper Junction, Arizona
- Toad Hop, Indiana
- Hoop and Holler, Texas
- Bug, Kentucky

- Big Ugly, West Virginia
- Soso, Mississippi
- Bumpass, Virginia
- Peculiar, Missouri
- Chugwater, Wyoming
- Yum Yum, Tennessee
- Cheesequake, New Jersey
- Bird in Hand, Penn.
- Possum Kingdom, Texas
- Pie Town, New Mexico
- Cookietown, Oklahoma
- Ninety Six, S. Carolina
- Chicken Bristle, Illinois
- Love Station, Tennessee
- Shaft Ox Corner, Del.
- Okay, Oklahoma (Okay, OK)

Check for yourself: Cats don't have eyelashes.

REEL WISDOM

*We go to movies to be entertained, but
occasionally we can be enlightened, too.*

"You know, Peter, with great power comes great responsibility."
—**Uncle Ben, *Spider-man***

"Never give up! Never surrender!"
—**Commander Taggart, *Galaxy Quest***

"The future is whatever you make it, so make it a good one."
—**Doc Brown, *Back to the Future, Part 3***

"Never send an adult to do a kid's job."
—**Carmen, *Spy Kids***

"There's some good in this world, Mr. Frodo, and it's worth fighting for."
—**Sam, *The Two Towers***

"Let your heart guide you. It whispers, so listen carefully."
—**Littlefoot's mother, *The Land Before Time***

"You can't stop change any more than you can stop the suns from setting."
—**Shmi Skywalker, *Star Wars: Episode I***

"It does not do to dwell on dreams, Harry, and forget to live."
—**Dumbledore, *Harry Potter & the Sorcerer's Stone***

"Some people without brains do an awful lot of talking."
—**The Scarecrow, *The Wizard of Oz***

PET PALS

*Sure, there are a lot of stories about dog heroes—but
what about rats, pigs, and raccoons? Read on.*

RAT ATTACK
In Stuttgart, Germany, the Steich family's pet
rat, Gerd, is a real hero. Gerd lived in a book-
case and normally was just a friendly, mild-mannered
pet. But one night two burglars broke into the house.
Surprise attack! With teeth bared and feet outstretched, Gerd landed on the face of one thug, practically scaring the life out of him. Then he pounced on
the other burglar's foot, scurried up his pant leg, and
gave him a ferocious bite...right where it counts. The
would-be burglars were caught. It turns out that they
were suspects in a series of robberies and murders, but
thanks to Gerd the hero rat, the Steich family was not
among their victims.

PIG PATROL

One day, a mentally handicapped boy named Anthony
went swimming in a lake near Houston, Texas. Suddenly he realized he had gone too far from shore and
started to panic. Anthony flailed around in the water,
then began to sink. Luckily, a friend's pet pig (her
name was Priscilla) heard the boy's cries for help and
swam out to save him. Anthony held onto the pig's
harness, and she towed him back to shore. The boy was

Have goats always been tame? Na-ah-ah-ah! They were domesticated around 7000 B.C.

saved, and the city of Houston declared the day, "Priscilla the Pig Day." Priscilla was later inducted into the Texas Pet Hall of Fame.

RACCOON RESCUE

Charley is a pet raccoon who lived with the Mertens family in northern Michigan. One night, while the family slept, their house caught on fire.

Charley raced into the parents' room, chattering wildly, and tugged at the father's foot to wake him. Mr. and Mrs. Mertens woke up and ran through the smoke-filled hall to their daughters' bedroom. But just as they entered the room, the floor started to give way behind them. Flames shot up from below.

"The baby!" Mrs. Mertens cried, pointing to the nursery across the flames. There was no way to reach it. The family raced to the window—luckily, their neighbors had seen the fire and placed a ladder against the wall to help them. As they climbed down the ladder, they shouted, "Please, someone save the baby!"

The neighbors broke into the blazing house and tried to climb the stairs, but it was too late. The stairs had collapsed. There was no way to get to the baby.

Just when everything looked hopeless, a black-and-gray fur ball came hurtling down from above. It was Charley! And in his mouth was the Mertens' baby! The child was saved, the family was reunited, and, as you can imagine, there wasn't a more treasured pet in northern Michigan than Charley the raccoon.

Of all the words in the English language, the word *set* has the most definitions.

THE BUG AWARDS

There are more than 1.25 million species of insects,
but these take the cake (sometimes for real)!

Heaviest: The goliath beetle of Africa is the sumo wrestler of bugs. It grows up to eight inches and can weigh as much as four ounces (the weight of a quarter-pound hamburger patty).

Longest: The stick insect of Borneo, which can grow to 14 inches long.

Oldest: Jewel beetles hold the record for longest-living bugs. Their larvae can live inside trees for more than 35 years before they finally emerge as adult beetles.

Strongest: The rhinoceros beetle, also known as the Hercules beetle, can carry more than 800 times its own weight. That's the equivalent of *you* being able to pick up a *house!*

Biggest Wingspan: The giant owlet moth has a wingspan of up to 18 inches—bigger than most birds.

Deadliest: The award for all-time deadliest bug goes to the anopheles mosquito. This malaria-carrying pest is responsible for more deaths than any other animal in world history.

Smallest: Battledore-wing fairy flies are teensy weensy wasps, only .0083 inches long—the size of the period at the end of this sentence.

The answer is 42. What's the question? How many dots are on a pair of dice?

DUMB CROOKS

*From the BRI's crime blotter, here's
proof that crime doesn't pay.*

WRONG PLACE, WRONG TIME

A not-too-observant man tried to rob a bank on the ground floor of a busy building in New York. If he had checked it out carefully before he decided to rob that particular bank, he might have known the FBI had offices there.

But he didn't. What's more, he picked the worst possible day to rob the place—payday! Why? Several armed FBI agents were waiting in line to deposit their paychecks. So when the foolish robber told the teller to put the money in the bag, he instantly heard the clicking of 15 guns behind him…and was quickly arrested.

TURN THE OTHER CHEEK

In a packed courtroom in Athens, Texas, Judge Jim Parsons sentenced 40-year-old Ray Mason to eight years in prison. But just before the police moved in to haul him off to jail, Mason yelled, "Hey, judge, look at this!" Then he pulled down his pants and mooned the judge—and everyone else in the courtroom. Judge Parsons was not amused. He charged Mason with contempt of court and gave him an extra six months in the can.

GAMES AROUND THE GLOBE

We had a lot of fun finding the games we put in our first Bathroom Reader for Kids Only—and judging by the letters we got, you had fun playing them. So here are some more.

GAME: Down, Down, Down

WHERE IT'S FROM: Australia

WHAT YOU NEED: A tennis ball

NUMBER OF PLAYERS: 2 or more

HOW YOU PLAY:

1. Players stand in a wide circle and begin tossing the ball continuously back and forth until someone drops it.

2. When the ball is dropped, everyone yells, "Down on one knee!" and the player who dropped the ball must kneel on one knee and play from there.

3. Continue tossing the ball back and forth. If the same player drops the ball a second time, yell out, "Down on two knees!" She is now kneeling throughout the game.

4. Continue tossing the ball. If "old but-terfingers" drops the ball again, everyone yells, "Down on one elbow!"

5. Continue tossing the ball. If she drops it a fourth time, she's "Down on two elbows!" (and still on her knees).

One large oak tree can drink as much as three bathtubs' worth of water every day.

6. If she drops it a fifth time, it's "Down on your chin!"

7. As other players drop the ball, they go through the same steps—down on one knee, then two knees, etc.

8. The players must continue to throw and catch the ball from whatever position they are in. The game ends when you're laughing so much you start rolling around, not catching the ball at all.

GAME: One-Legged Rabbit (*Gradai Kha Dee-o*)
WHERE IT'S FROM: Thailand
WHAT YOU NEED: A field or gym
NUMBER OF PLAYERS: 10 or more
HOW YOU PLAY:

1. The players split up into two equal groups. One group is the Rabbits. The other group must remain within an area that has been marked out as the "Rabbit Hole."

2. One Rabbit hops on one foot into the Rabbit Hole and tries to touch as many members of the other team as she can, while hopping.

3. Players in the Rabbit Hole are out if they are touched

In Japan, kids get only six weeks of summer vacation.

or if they cross the boundary. The Rabbit is out if she puts two legs down or changes legs.

4. However, if she is tired, the Rabbit can hop back to the start line and pick another Rabbit to take her place.

5. The game's over when no one is left in the Rabbit Hole.

GAME: Pebble Tag
WHERE IT'S FROM: Greece
WHAT YOU NEED: A small
pebble and a large field
NUMBER OF PLAYERS: 5 or more
HOW YOU PLAY:

1. Select someone to be "It." "It" then chooses and marks a goal about 30 feet away.

2. The others line up and hold their hands out in front of them, palms together and thumbs pointing up, with a little opening at the top of their hands, forming a cup.

3. "It" walks down the line and drops (or pretends to drop) the pebble into someone's hand.

4. The person receiving the pebble must run to the goal without being tagged by the other players—or the person may pretend like he didn't get it. Players watch each other, trying to figure out who has the pebble.

5. But the person with the pebble can't fake it forever—he must run before "It" reaches the end of the line.

6. If the person gets to the goal and back to "It" *without* being tagged, he's the next "It." If he's tagged, then the person who tagged him is "It."

IMAGINARY WORLDS

*Here's a fun little quiz: match the imaginary place
with the book or movie it came from. Bonus question:
Which one is also the name of a real place?*

Place Names	Titles
1. Hogwarts	a. *Gulliver's Travels*
2. Never-Never Land	b. *The Lord of the Rings*
3. Camelot	c. *The Lion, the Witch and the Wardrobe*
4. Thousand Acre Wood	d. *The White Dragon*
5. Pern	e. *Harry Potter*
6. Wild Island	f. *Dracula*
7. Narnia	g. *Winnie the Pooh*
8. Lilliput	h. *Star Wars*
9. Middle Earth	i. *The Wizard of Oz*
10. Gotham City	j. *My Father's Dragon*
11. Tatooine	k. *Peter Pan*
12. Emerald City	l. *The Once and Future King*
13. Transylvania	m. *Batman*

Answers

1. e; 2. k; 3. l; 4. g; 5. d; 6. j; 7. c; 8. a; 9. b; 10. m; 11. h; 12. i; 13. f. Bonus question: Transylvania.

The movie *Titanic* takes 40 minutes longer to watch than the actual ship took to sink.

MAY I TAKE YOUR ORDER?

Some of your favorite foods come from other countries. Hamburgers and hot dogs originated in Germany; pizza is Italian. So if you like those...

May We Suggest: Bangers and mash
What Is It? It's part of a British lunch or dinner. A banger is a type of sausage, a bit plumper and curvier than a hot dog and quite a bit spicier. It's usually pan-fried or deep-fried in batter. "Mash" is short for mashed potatoes.

For breakfast, the British love rashers (bacon), black pudding (a kind of sausage), white pudding (another kind of sausage), eggs, stewed tomatoes, and kidneys.

May We Suggest: Spotted dick
What Is It? It's a dessert. The earliest recipes for it appeared in England in 1847. To make it, take a flat sheet of dough, cover it with sugar and raisins, then roll it up and boil or bake it. *Voilà!* You've got spotted dick.

May We Suggest: Haggis, neeps, and tatties
What Is It? It's the national dish of Scotland. And people either love it or hate it. Haggis is actually a sheep's stomach stuffed with all of the other internal

---

Six official languages of the U.N.: Arabic, Chinese, English, French, Spanish, and Russian.

parts of the sheep mixed with ground oatmeal. It's sort
of like a huge sausage. It's traditionally served on New
Year's Eve with neeps and tatties (mashed turnips and
mashed potatoes).

May We Suggest: Poi
What Is It? It's a Hawaiian side dish—a starchy gray
pudding that is made from the root of the taro plant
(which looks something like a hairy potato). Many
people around the world eat taro, but only the Hawai-
ians make poi. One description of poi is that it tastes
"like library paste…without the flavor." Some Hawai-
ians like it fresh, but many prefer day-old poi, when it's
a little sour. The best way to eat it is with your fingers.
In fact, poi consistency is measured by how many fingers you need to scoop up a mouthful. Two-fingered poi
is considered *ono!* (The best!)

May We Suggest: Blood pudding
What Is It? It's another kind of pudding…one made
with blood—lots of it. Blood pudding was first made in
the days when people slaughtered their own hogs. Not
wanting to waste any part of the pig, they saved the
blood and mixed it with raisins, sugar, nuts, cooked
rice, oranges, figs, and spices. Then the mixture was
baked in the oven and served warm. It may not be as
popular as it once was, but blood pudding is still considered a holiday classic in England, Ireland, and
French Canadian provinces.

A mosquito can drink more than $1\frac{1}{2}$ times its own weight in blood.

MOVIE BLOOPERS

Movies may seem well-thought-out, but if you look carefully, you can find all kinds of goofs and flubs. Here are a few we found in some hit films.

Movie: *Star Wars, Episode II: Attack of the Clones* (2002)
Scene: Packing for her trip to Naboo, Padme is in her closet holding a red garment.
Blooper: A moment later, when she places it in her suitcase, the garment has changed to blue.

Movie: *Lord of the Rings: The Fellowship of the Ring* (2001)
Scene: Gandalf visits Bilbo Baggins.
Blooper: Gandalf's belt repeatedly switches between being tied and untied as he speaks to Bilbo.

Movie: *The Princess Diaries* (2001)
Scene: Mia and her grandmother are standing by some telescopes when Mia takes a bite out of a corndog. A few seconds later, she offers her grandmother a bite.
Blooper: The corndog is whole again.

Movie: *Spider-Man* (2002)
Scene: Mary Jane is being mugged by four men. Spider-Man throws two of the men through the two windows behind Mary Jane. Then the camera goes back to Spider-Man beating up the other two guys.

First product to have a UPC bar code: Wrigley's Juicy Fruit gum.

Blooper: When the camera goes back to Mary Jane, the two windows aren't broken.

Movie: *Beauty and the Beast* (1991)
Scene: In the beginning of the movie, Belle sits down by a fountain with a book. A sheep takes a bite out of a page in the book. The page has a picture on it.
Blooper: Later in the movie, Gaston says, "How can you read this? It doesn't even have any pictures!"

Movie: *Dr. Dolittle* (1998)
Scene: Dr. Dolittle gets out of bed to answer the door. He turns on a light switch and opens the door.
Blooper: There's no switch—he's flicking the wall!

Movie: *Scooby Doo* (2001)
Scene: While Fred is a zombie, he punches through a window and grabs Shaggy by the neck.
Blooper: Fred was a very safe zombie—you can clearly see the tape on his arm protecting him from the glass.

Movie: *Aladdin* (on the 1993 video copies of the film)
Scene: Aladdin is on the flying carpet just off Princess Jasmine's balcony. She is seen behind the curtain.
Blooper: A strange voice whispers something. But what? Some people claim it's "take off your clothes." The people at Disney say it's "take off and go"...but just to be safe, they removed the line from later video and DVD versions.

The IQ of an average stutterer is 14 points higher than a non-stutterer.

COOKING WITH UNCLE JOHN

What do you say we make a big bowl of snot? What ingredients are used to make fake snot? Pretty much the same ones that make real snot: protein, sugar, and water. Now, let's get cooking!

BOOGIE MAN

FAKE SNOT
Ingredients:
- three packages of unflavored gelatin (the protein)
- light corn syrup (the sugar)
- about ½ cup water

Recipe: You'll need an adult to help you with this recipe. First, heat the water in a pan until it boils. Remove it from the heat and sprinkle in the packages of gelatin. Let this mixture soften a few minutes and then stir it with a fork. Add enough corn syrup to make 1 cup of thin, goopy glop. Stir the glop with the fork. While you're stirring it, lift the fork to pull out long strands of snot. As the "snot" begins to cool, it will thicken. Add more water, if you need to, a spoonful at a time, to keep it nice and slimy.

EXTRA BONUS: FAKE BOOGERS!

You can make fake boogers, too. Real boogers are formed when mucus coats a tiny dust particle in your nose and then dries out and hardens.

That's how you make fake boogers, too. Just take the fake snot, toss in about a pinch of dust and... *eureka!* You've got fake boogers! Now go wipe one on a wall. You could even put one in your friend's sandwich...

* * *

HE'S GONNA BLOW!

When you have a cold, you just reach for a box of tissue to help you with your snotty noses. But before there were disposable tissues, people carried handkerchiefs, or "snot rags"—a practice that started more than 2,000 years ago in Rome.

Of course, people didn't always use hankies. Many people just wiped their noses on their sleeves. But in the 1500s King Francis I of France thought it was gross and decided to put a stop to the filthy habit. He ordered buttons sewn on all men's coat sleeves to make them use their handkerchiefs instead of their sleeves. In the 1700s, Admiral Nelson had buttons sewn on the sleeves of all all British naval uniforms for the same reason, as did Napoleon for the French military in the 1800s.

And that's why men's coats have buttons on their sleeves today.

HOW ROCK GROUPS GOT THEIR NAMES

If you ask most rock bands, they'll tell you that finding a good name can be as hard as making good music. Sometimes the perfect name just appears—others take years to find.

Good Charlotte named themselves after a children's book about a little girl named Charlotte who is bullied all the time. But her nanny loves her a lot and calls her "good Charlotte." (The band can't stand the book.)

Puddle of Mudd got their name after the Missouri River flooded their practice space and turned the floor into a big "puddle of mud."

Matchbox 20 came up with their name when drummer Paul Doucette was a waiter in a diner. One day he saw a customer wearing a #20 softball shirt. It was covered with patches, and the only word he could read was "Matchbox."

Foo Fighters. Founder Dave Grohl has always been fascinated with UFOs. He named his band after the mysterious fireballs seen by American pilots in WWII (see page 259). He also named the band's label Roswell, in honor of Roswell, New Mexico, the site of a famous UFO "crash" in 1947 (see page 41).

No kidding: Kid Rock's real name is Bobby Ritchie.

No Doubt. When the band formed in 1986, they wanted to call themselves Apple Core. But they also liked the phrase that their original lead singer, John Spence, would always say: "No doubt." Sadly, Spence died in 1987. When 18-year-old Gwen Stefani took over as lead singer, the band took the name No Doubt as a tribute to him.

Sugar Ray. They first called themselves the Tories, then the Shrinky Dinx, after a toy made by Hasbro. But Hasbro didn't like the group using their product name and threatened to sue them. So the group decided to change their name to Sugar Ray, in honor of the band's favorite boxer, Sugar Ray Leonard.

Moby was born Richard Melville Hall. His great-great-grand uncle was Herman Melvile, who wrote *Moby Dick*. Moby's parents honored his famous ancestor by giving him the nickname of the infamous white whale.

Sixpence None the Richer named themselves after a passage from C. S. Lewis's book *Mere Christianity*.

Blink 182 was originally just called "Blink." The band was forced to change the name when an Irish techno band—also called Blink—threatened to sue them. Although there are countless rumors of what the "182" stands for, ranging from the number of times certain words are said in movies, to numbers that relate to where they live, the truth is it's really just a number they chose at random and thought sounded good.

Keep at it! *Harry Potter* author J. K. Rowling started writing stories when she was 6.

BATHROOM INVENTIONS

*Uncle John thought you'd like to know the history
of a few things found in the his favorite room.*

RUBBER DUCKY, YOU'RE THE ONE

This bright yellow bath pal first appeared in the mid-1800s when the New York Rubber Company started manufacturing rubber squeak toys. But it would be more than 100 years before rubber duckies became popular. Who do we have to thank for that? Ernie the Muppet. In 1970 he sang the song "Rubber Ducky" on *Sesame Street*…and suddenly every kid wanted one.

TOOTHBRUSHES

Ever heard of a "chew stick"? A chew stick is a small twig with one end frayed into a brushlike tuft of wood fiber. That's what people used before there were toothbrushes. So where did toothbrushes come from? China. The Chinese invented brushes made of hog hair in the 1400s. But these *bristle* brushes weren't commonly used for teeth cleaning in Europe until an Englishman named William Addis "reinvented" them in 1780.

Toothbrushes aren't made of hog hair anymore. Since DuPont introduced Dr. West's Miracle Toothbrush in 1938, they've been constructed of a more hygienic, longer-lasting, and easier-to-manufacture fiber: nylon.

TOWELS

No one knows exactly when towels were invented. We do know that drying cloths made of linen were used in ancient Rome and in ancient Japan. Today most towels are made of terrycloth, a cotton fabric invented in France in 1841. Another fascinating towel fact: Studies show that clean towels start to smell bad after a couple of days of use, even though they only touch clean skin. Why? Because dead skin cells stick to the moist towel, which is the ideal environment for the growth of mildew. Yech!

THERMOMETERS

Galileo invented the thermometer around 1590. But those early thermometers were primarily used to measure air temperature.

Then in 1866 an inventor came up with the first thermometer that could be used for taking a person's body temperature. His name? Thomas C. *Allbutt*. Really.

Before Allbutt's invention, the only temperature-taking contraptions for people were more than a foot long and required the patient to put the bulb in his mouth for at least 20 minutes. So instead, doctors (or mothers) would place their hand on the patient's forehead and make their best guess. But Allbutt's invention changed all that. It was as thin as a pencil, six inches long, and only took five minutes to get an accurate reading.

Dumb question: What do *benighted, nescient,* and *imbecilic* mean? "Dumb."

RIDDLE ME THIS

Q: What makes smoke come out of Uncle John's ears?
A: Trying to answer these classic riddles.

Q: What falls but never breaks?

A: Night!

Q: While walking across a bridge I saw a boat full of people. Yet on the boat there wasn't a single person. Why?

A: Everyone on the boat was married!

Q: I am the beginning of eternity,
The end of time and space;
The beginning of every end,
And the end of every place.
What am I?

A: The letter E!

Q: You are the bus driver. At the first stop, 4 people get on. At the second stop, 8 people get on. At the third stop, 2 people get off, and at the last stop, everyone gets off. What color are the bus driver's eyes?

A: The riddle starts out by saying you are the bus driver. So what color are your eyes?

Q: Railroad crossing—look out for the cars. Can you spell that without any R's?

A: T-H-A-T!

Q: Pronounced as one letter but written with three. Only two different letters are used to make me. I'm double, I'm single, I'm black, blue, and gray. I'm read from both ends and the same either way.

A: Eye!

KIDS CAN...

*Some ideas are so good you wonder why no one
thought of them before. But one thing is for certain:
there's no age limit on a great idea. Here are
three great ones from three remarkable kids.*

KIDS F.A.C.E.
Melissa Poe was 9 years old when she started
Kids for a Clean Environment (Kids F.A.C.E)
at Percy Priest Elementary in Nashville, Tennessee, in
1989. The original club—Melissa and five of her
friends—began recycling, picking up litter, planting
trees, and inviting other kids to join them. Then Melissa wrote this letter to President George H. W. Bush:

> Dear Mr. President,
> Please do something about pollution. I want to live till I am
> 100 years old. Mr. President, if you ignore this letter, we will
> all die of pollution. Please help!

The president didn't respond, but Melissa didn't give
up. She got a local advertising company to reproduce
her letter on a billboard (for free). Then she appeared
on *The Today Show*. From that she was able to get her
letter displayed on 250 more billboards across the country. Soon, letters started coming in from kids around
the country, asking how they could join her club and
help save the environment.

From the original six kids, the club has now grown
to more than 300,000 members from 23 different coun-

tries. And they *are* helping to save the environment—they've distributed and planted over a million trees!

SUITCASES FOR KIDS

Aubyn Burnside was 10 years old in 1996 when she got her great idea. Her older sister Leslie was a social worker who placed foster children in new homes. One day Leslie told Aubyn that some kids were so poor they had to carry their belongings in plastic trash bags instead of suitcases.

Aubyn couldn't get the image out of her mind: kids throwing their dolls, their favorite T-shirts, and their teddy bears into ugly black plastic bags. She knew how that would make her feel—like she didn't matter.

Just In Case

Aubyn made up her mind to get every one of those foster kids their own suitcase. She started by looking in her attic to see if her family had any extras. Then she contacted her local church and 4-H club and asked them to help her. She called her idea Suitcases for Kids.

She spread the word to Sunday schools, businesses, and the Boy Scouts and Girl Scouts. Result: within a month, Aubyn had collected hundreds of suitcases. First she gave them out to foster kids in her state. Then calls began to come in from other states. Foster kids all over America need-

The Barnum and Bailey Circus is the world's longest-running circus.

ed suitcases. By the end of the year, Aubyn had collected and donated more than 4,000 suitcases!

Now, Aubyn works with her brother out of their home in North Carolina. Together they've helped start Suitcases for Kids organizations in every state in America, in Canada, and in 10 other countries.

KIDS CAN FREE THE CHILDREN

Kids Can Free the Children was created by 12-year-old Craig Kielburger, of Thornhill, Ontario, in 1995. Craig had read a newspaper article about the abuse of kids working in Pakistan. He learned that 250 million children around the world were forced to work. No school, no play—just work. That made him so angry that he decided to do something about it.

He started a program called Free the Children—a network of children helping other children around the world. They run petition drives and letter-writing campaigns. And they raise money. So far, Free the Children has built more than 300 primary schools worldwide providing daily education to 15,000 children. They've also shipped more than $2.5 million worth of medical supplies to clinics in poorer countries.

This organization is run by children...for children. Adults work as volunteer staff, but have no decision-making power. Only kids can vote and set policies.

Want to contact one of these groups and start to make a difference? For more information, check out our RESOURCE GUIDE on page 284.

Looney law: It's illegal for cats to drink beer in Natchez, Mississippi.

CANDY BITS

A few facts about candy—short and sweet.

POP ROCKS. In 1956 a chemist for General Foods was looking for a way to make instant carbonated soda pop by trapping carbon dioxide in hard candy tablets. One afternoon he popped some of the experimental nuggets into his mouth...and felt them pop. No one at General Foods could think of a use for the substance, so it was shelved for almost 20 years. But in 1975 it was rediscovered and introduced as Pop Rocks—and became the hottest-selling candy in history. More than 500 million packets were sold between 1975 and 1980.

PEZ. Invented in 1927 by Eduard Haas, an Austrian antismoking advocate who marketed peppermint-flavored PEZ as a cigarette substitute. The candy gets its name from the German word for peppermint, *Pfefferminze*. Haas brought it to the United States in 1952. It bombed, so he reintroduced it as a children's toy, complete with cartoon heads and fruity flavors.

CHARLESTON CHEW. Sometimes the names of candy bars come from the fads that are popular when they are introduced. The Charleston Chew was introduced during the Roaring Twenties, and was named after the latest dance craze, the Charleston.

BLACK CROWS. The Mason Candy Co. decided to

introduce a new candy in the 1890s. The licorice-fla-vored gumdrops were supposed to be called Black Rose. But the printer misunderstood the instructions and printed the wrappers with the name "Black Crows." He refused to redo the job, claiming it was Mason's mis-take. Rather than pay to reprint the wrappers, the folks at Mason decided to change the name of the product. Black Crows are still available by that name today.

MEXICAN HATS. When Mexican Hats candies were introduced by Heide (makers of Jujyfruits and Gummi Bears) they were called "Wet 'ems and Wear 'ems." Kids were supposed to lick the candies (which are in the shape of hats) and stick them to their foreheads. Why the candy company wanted kids to wear the candies is unknown.

KRAFT CARAMELS. During the Great Depression of the 1930s, James L. Kraft started making caramels. He didn't particularly like candy—he just needed another product for his cheese salesmen to sell. The candy suc-ceeded because grocers wanted a summer substitute for chocolate, which melted in the heat.

THREE MUSKETEERS. Advertising in the 1950s suggested that the Three Musketeers candy bar got its name because it was big enough for three people to share. The truth is, it was originally made of three sepa-rate nougat sections: vanilla, chocolate, and strawberry. Eventually, the strawberry and vanilla nougat sections were eliminated, leaving only the chocolate nougat.

Horse riding is believed to be at least 5,000 years old.

HOW DO SUPERSTITIONS START?

Sometimes the origin of a custom can be more interesting than the custom itself.

Superstition: It's important to say "God bless you" when someone sneezes.

Why We Believe It: It was once considered good luck to sneeze. It meant that evil was being expelled from your body. Then, in 590 A.D., a terrible plague swept through Europe and many people became very sick, some sneezing violently. Most people who got the plague died, so sneezing soon became identified with impending doom. Pope Gregory the Great passed a law on February 16, 600 A.D. that required everyone to ask God to bless the sneezer.

Superstition: If you spill salt, bad luck will come your way.

Why We Believe It: A long time ago, salt was considered very valuable—more precious than gold. Why? Because it could preserve meat, flavor foods, and even cure illnesses. It was very important to never waste it. If you did spill some salt, it meant the devil was close at

The term *plus* in mathematics is short for *surplus*.

hand. To scare him away, you would toss a pinch of the spilled salt over your left shoulder. If you had really good aim, you'd hit him in the eye.

Superstition: Step on a crack, break your mother's back. (Or: Step on a line, break your father's spine.)
Why We Believe It: People used to think that lines and cracks in the earth were gateways to other worlds. To step on a crack was a very scary thing because your soul could slip through it into the underworld. Or worse yet, the underworld could reach up and hurt a member of your family, like your mother or your father.

Superstition: Walking under a ladder is bad luck.
Why We Believe It: You might think that it's obvious why walking under a ladder is considered bad luck—a hammer or a can of paint could fall on your head. This makes sense, but it's not the reason. The real reason has its roots in ancient Egypt, where people believed that triangles represented their three most sacred gods and thus had special powers. If you walked through the triangle formed by a ladder leaning against a wall, you were defying the gods.

Is there anything you can do to ward off bad luck if you accidentally walk under a ladder? The Romans would make a fist, with the thumb protruding between the index and middle fingers, and thrust it toward the ladder. It was called the sign of the *fico* and was thought to ward off bad luck.

Pantophobes are afraid of everything.

ROSWELL

*More than 50 years after America's most famous
UFO encounter, people are still asking:
What really happened out there?*

WAS IT A METEOR?
On July 4, 1947, a bright light shot across
the sky over Roswell, New Mexico. It
exploded and fell to earth on a ranch outside of town.
At first, townspeople thought it was a meteor that had
crashed. Several men rushed to see what it was.

WAS IT A SPACESHIP?

One of the first to arrive was a team of archaeologists
who happened to be working in the area. They quickly
discovered that this was no meteor. According to newspaper accounts, the object looked like "an airplane
without wings." As they approached it, they saw three
strange bodies. Two were on the ground and one was
visible through a hole in the side of the craft.

WHAT WAS THAT STRANGE MATERIAL?

Rancher "Mac" Brazel came across more pieces of the
wreckage of the crash in his pasture. Bits of shiny metal
were scattered across his field. The metal was like nothing Brazel had ever seen before. It was as soft as cloth,
yet he couldn't cut it with a knife or burn it. He showed
the strange material to some neighbors, then alerted the

sheriff in Roswell, who notified the U.S. Air Force.

WHY DID THE AIR FORCE SAY IT WAS A SPACESHIP?

Over the next few days, the Air Force cleared away the wreckage. On July 8, they issued a press release announcing that a flying saucer had crashed in Roswell. But the next day, the government changed the story—they now said they had been mistaken and that it was only a crashed weather balloon.

WHAT HAPPENED TO THE BODIES?

Strange stories soon began popping up. There were reports that the Air Force had removed some bodies with "large eyes and strange faces" from the crash scene. People began to talk about a place called Area 51 in Nevada, where the bodies were rumored to have been taken.

Area 51 is a top-secret military facility 90 miles north of Las Vegas. The number refers to a block of land, at the center of which is a large air base. Area 51 is America's foremost testing ground for secret aircraft. It is heavily guarded and the Air Force refuses to discuss what goes on there.

Hot stuff! The center of the sun is estimated to be 59,000,000°F.

WHAT WERE THE BODIES?

When asked about the bodies, government spokesmen said the bodies were actually crash dummies used to test parachutes that fell out of the weather balloon. As far as the Air Force was concerned, the case was closed.

UNANSWERED QUESTIONS

Dozens of people witnessed the crash at Roswell. Would all of them lie about what they saw? Why would the Air Force say a spaceship had crashed and then deny it? We may never hear the real truth, because that information is

CLASSIFIED

*   *   *

DOG'S BEST FRIEND

"On my block a lot of people walk their dogs and I always see them walking along with their little poop bags. This, to me, is the lowest activity in human life. Following a dog with a little scooper. Waiting for him to go so you can walk down the street with it in your bag. If aliens are watching this through telescopes, they're going to think the dogs are the leaders of the planet. If you see two life forms, one of them's making a poop, the other one's carrying it for him, who would you assume is in charge?"

—Jerry Seinfeld

The first comic strip to become a feature film, *The Mark of Zorro* (1920).

WILD SPITTERS

Ready... set... H-O-C-C-CHHHHH!

S PITTING CAMELS
Next time you're at the zoo, you might be tempt-
ed to walk right up to a camel. Bad idea. If a
camel gets annoyed, it'll hock a huge, green lugie at
you! And this isn't saliva—it's the partially digested
contents of the camel's stomach. It smells so foul that
you'll be running for the shower... so keep your distance.

SPITTING SPIDERS

Some spiders build webs to ensnare their prey. Others
move very fast, easily overcoming any insect. But not
the spitting spider of northern Mexico. Instead, it waits
until nighttime, when most insects are at rest. Then it
sneaks up on a potential meal and *pitooey!* It spits a poisonous sticky substance in a zigzag pattern all over its
prey, instantly immobilizing it. Dinner is served!

SPITTING SNAKES

An Asian viper called a spitting cobra kills its prey like
every other poisonous snake: by injecting venom through
its fangs. But it has another trick as well: it can spray
venom from its fangs—not to kill, but to injure potential
predators. This spitter aims for the eyes, to cause blind-
ness. And because it has very good aim, it can spit its
venom from up to 10 feet away and still score a bull's-eye.

Human saliva contains an antiseptic that kills germs.

HIIIIIIIII-YA!

Have you ever seen a karate expert break a board with one chop of his hand? How about split a brick in two with a kick? Okay, how about an entire house?

DEMOLITION SQUAD

It was a gray morning in Bradford, England, when a team of 15 karate experts gathered to bring down their toughest opponent yet: a six-room, 150-year-old house.

As the team did warm-up exercises, dozens of curious onlookers gathered to witness the spectacle. When the warm-up was done, the karate team lined up in front of the house and awaited the attack command from their *sensei*, (a martial arts teacher) Phil Milner. Everyone was silent. Finally the command was given and the demolition began.

CRRRRR-ACK!

That old house didn't have a chance. Methodically, the team broke board after board, brick after brick—all with their bare hands and feet. Well, almost all. The stone fireplace was stubborn and seemingly unbreakable. Despite relentless pummeling, it stood solidly. The experts finally decided they needed something stronger than a hand, so some members of the team volunteered to use…their heads. The volunteers were picked up and used as human battering rams. The fireplace was toast!

The word *karate* is Japanese for "empty hand."

As amazing as it was for the crowd of 200 to see this demolition, it was even more incredible to hear it. The team emitted loud grunts and *hiiiii-yas*, and the house groaned in protest as the wood split and the bricks crumbled. All of this, combined with the cheers of the spectators, made for one of the most bizarre—and loudest—sporting events in history.

WINNERS BY A KNOCKOUT

Many hours later, the house was reduced to a pile of rubble. The demolishers were bruised and dusty, but still standing. As a final gesture to their defeated opponent, Phil Milner and his team of karate experts faced the ruins…and bowed.

According to scientists, all warm-blooded animals dream—except dolphins and spiny anteaters.

ASK THE EXPERTS

*Everyone's got a question or two they'd like
answered. Here are a few classic questions
with answers from top trivia experts.*

SUPER FLY

Q: *How do flies walk upside down on the ceiling?*

A: A fly has six legs. On each leg there are two
little claws that look sort of like a lobster's claw. Underneath the claws are a pair of small fuzzy pads called *pul-
villi*. These are suction pads, which the fly presses to the
surface to squeeze out the air, creating enough suction
to hold itself up. (From *How Do Flies Walk Upside
Down?*)

GOOSEBUMPS

Q: *Why do people get goosebumps?*

A: There was a time (ages ago) when the human body
was covered with thick hair. When it got cold, the
hairs would stand on end, keeping the cold air out and
the warm air in. The hairs have long since disappeared,
but the place where the hair used to be still bristles,
trying to get warm. (From *The Book of Answers*)

BIRD POOP

Q: *What's that black dot in the middle of bird droppings?*

A: The black dot is poop. The white part is urine.

Q: What's the most popular topping for a Domino's Pizza in Japan?   A: Squid.

They come out together, at the same time, out of the same hole. The white stuff, which is slightly sticky, clings to the black stuff. (From *Why Do Clocks Run Clockwise?*)

RUMBLY IN THE TUMBLY

Q: *Why does your stomach growl?*

A: Every 75 to 115 minutes, your stomach's muscles contract. If there is no food present, the stomach creates a wavelike motion that causes the air and your digestive gases to roll around and create that rumbling sound. That rumble becomes your own personal lunchtime bell, which can be totally embarrassing. (From *Why Can't You Tickle Yourself?*)

SEE YOU IN MY DREAMS

Q: *Do people who are born blind ever dream?*

A: People who are blind from birth do dream, but they don't dream the same visual images as sighted people. Said one man who has been blind since birth, "my dreams are never with shapes or colors. I dream about touching things. Once I dreamed I was being chased by someone with a gun and felt as if the bullets were actually piercing my back." So rather than see shapes, textures, and colors, they hear and feel the dream.

It is also interesting that people who can see and become blind later in life will still see images in their dreams. However, the images tend to fade the longer they remain blind. (From *Do Fish Drink Water?*)

GHOST SHIP

Of all of history's unsolved mysteries, perhaps none is stranger than the fateful voyage of the Mary Celeste.

SAILING INTO THE UNKNOWN

On November 5, 1872, a ship named the *Mary Celeste* set sail from New York bound for Genoa, Italy, under the command of Captain Benjamin Briggs. On board were a crew of seven along with the captain's wife and their two-year-old daughter.

A month later, on the morning of December 4, the *Mary Celeste* sailed out of the fog off the coast of Spain and was spotted by the crew of the British ship *Dei Gratia*. The *Mary Celeste*'s sails were raised and the hull and masts appeared in good order. The crew of the *Dei Gratia* hailed the ship, but received no answer, so they boarded her, ready to extend their greetings. What they found was mystifying: the ship was completely deserted.

ANYBODY HOME?

The ship's cargo—1,700 barrels of alcohol—was untouched. The money box was full. There was plenty of food and water. In fact, some reports tell of finding a meal on the table, as if dinner had just been served. Toys were found on the captain's bed, as if his little daughter had just played with them. Everyone's clothes were still on board. The only things missing were nautical charts and maps, a lifeboat…and all the people.

Rainy-day fact: Umbrellas were originally invented to keep the sun off.

Where did everybody go?

WHAT HAPPENED?

The mysterious disappearance of the *Mary Celeste*'s crew had people all over the world wondering.

• Some believed the crew mutinied, murdered the captain and his family, then took the ship. But if that were true, why did they abandon it?

• Perhaps pirates attacked the ship and killed everyone aboard. But that made no sense because nothing was stolen.

• The most outrageous explanation offered was that the ship had been attacked by a giant squid. But a squid wouldn't have been interested in the ship's papers. And a squid wouldn't need a lifeboat.

Eeek! There are 29,000 different species of spiders.

A POSSIBLE EXPLANATION

The mystery of the *Mary Celeste* has puzzled people for over a century. In all that time, say experts, only one reasonable explanation has been proposed. According to this theory, four things happened, in succession:

1. The captain died of natural causes while the ship was caught in bad weather.

2. A crew member misread the depth of the water in the hold, and everyone thought the ship was sinking.

3. They panicked and abandoned ship in such a hurry that they took no food or water.

4. Everyone in the lifeboat eventually starved or drowned.

Is that what happened? Could be…
but no one will ever know.

*　　*　　*

DUMB JOKES

Q: Why do hummingbirds hum?
A: Because they don't know the words.

Q: How can you find a lost rabbit?
A: Make a noise like a carrot.

Q: Why is a pig's tail like getting up at five in the morning?
A: It's twirly. (Don't get it? Say it slowly.)

LIFE ON THE EDGE

*Here at the BRI we love hearing stories about brave
dogs. Good old Roy may be the bravest yet.*

P**LAYTIME CATASTROPHE**
The Rongemo family lived up on the third floor
of an apartment building in Sweden. One day,
Mr. Rongemo went into the kitchen to help his wife,
while his two-year-old daughter played in the living
room. When Mr. Rongemo returned to the living room,
he saw that the window was open and his daughter was
gone. He ran to the window and nearly fainted from
fright. His little girl was outside, crawling on all fours
along a narrow ledge that circled the building!

ROY TO THE RESCUE!
But the girl wasn't alone: following just behind her was
the family's German Shepherd, Roy, whining softly with
distress. Both the dog and the baby were out of Mr.
Rongemo's reach. Worse yet, there was no room on the
narrow ledge for either of them to turn around to get
back to the window.

Mr. Rongemo knew that if he crawled out after
them, he would probably startle the baby and the dog,
and then all three of them would probably fall and die.
Still, he had to do *something*! So he told his wife to stay
at the window while he raced down to the street to try
to catch his daughter, just in case.

The baby continued to crawl farther and farther away from the window, with Roy the dog following right behind her. On the street below, a crowd had gathered. People were frantically trying to put together a makeshift net to catch the baby if she fell. But the net turned out to be unnecessary.

A NARROW ESCAPE

To everyone's amazement, Roy suddenly grabbed the baby's diaper with his teeth. He then started walking backward, very carefully pulling the little girl back to the window, inch by inch.

The heart-pounding journey took three minutes, until Mrs. Rongemo could finally catch hold of her little daughter. She pulled the baby inside, and Roy leapt into the room behind her, proudly wagging his tail.

This amazing story has an amazing ending, too: The Rongemo family had been thinking of giving Roy away. They were worried that he was too big for such a little child. Think this brave dog got to stay with the family? You bet!

Chicago comes from *checagou*, the Algonquin Indian name for the onions that grew there.

BRAINTEASERS

Put on your thinking caps (or whatever else you like to wear that makes you feel smarter)! Answers are on page 282.

1. Apples and oranges. Rebecca, George, and Helen are eating oranges. Fred, Karen, and Dave are eating apples. To which group does Steve belong? (*Hint:* Look at the names.)

2. Chop shop. There are only two barbers in a small town. One has a neat haircut and a clean shop. The other has scraggly hair and a filthy shop with hair all over the floor. Which barber do you choose?

3. A fine find. A famous archaeologist claimed he discovered a rare gold coin with a marking on it that said 458 B.C. People knew he was lying. How did they know?

4. Dollars and sense. Inside your wallet are six bills that total $63. None of them are $1 bills. What are the denominations of the bills?

5. Light Speed. Sam turned off his bedroom light and went to bed. The light switch is 10 feet away, yet he got into bed before the room got dark. How is that possible?

6. Soaked. Four men dove into a swimming pool, but only three of them got their hair wet. Why?

7. A-quiz. If a man is born in Alabama, grows up in Alaska, vacations in Albania, and dies in Africa, what is he?

SPARK IN THE DARK

Here's a science experiment you can do for little more than a buck.

What You Need:
- Pack of Wint-O-Green Lifesavers
- Very dark room or closet

What You Do:

1. Go into the room (take a friend or a mirror).
2. Bite into the Lifesaver. Whoa! It sparks.

You just discovered triboluminescence! What? *Tribo-luminescence* is light produced by striking or rubbing two special substances together. The electrons in the atoms of each substance are like little sponges absorbing the energy from the friction. When the friction stops, they release the energy...and it becomes light.

Do you have to use a Wint-O-Green Lifesaver? No. It will work with some other substances, but Wint-O-Greens work best. Why? They contain wintergreen oil, (methyl salicylate), which is actually fluorescent.

Pop blows its top! Want to create a soda volcano? Here's another experiment. Open a brand-new two-liter bottle of soda pop and drop in three or four Wint-O-Green Lifesavers. *Don't replace the cap.* When the carbon dioxide (CO_2) in the soda meets the Lifesavers, it will make big bubbles that will shoot out of the soda bottle. *Warning!* Do this trick in the kitchen sink or shower!

Geography quiz: How many countries are there in the world? As of 2003, there are 193.

REAL-LIFE X-MEN

It's hard to believe, but just like the X-Men in the comic books, these people are able to fire lightning bolts with a gesture, move furniture with a look, and read minds.

ELECTRON GIRL

*E*LECTRON GIRL **Jennie Morgan** of Sedalia, Missouri, could shoot sparks from her fingertips. These highly charged sparks were strong enough to knock people over. They could even knock people unconscious. Animals could sense this 14-year-old's electrical power and would stay far away from her. (Who would blame them?)

THE MAGNETIC KIDS

Caroline Clare, a teenager from Canada, was ill for nearly 18 months. The illness was bizarre, and doctors were unable to diagnose it. But even stranger: it turned Caroline into a living magnet. Metal objects, like forks and knives, stuck to her skin. Caroline was so magnetized that she was unable to pull the metal objects off herself. Someone (unmagnetized) had to do it for her.

Inga Gaiduchenko of Russia was 14 when she demonstrated her magnetic abilities to members of the

Moscow Technological Institute. They watched in amazement as spoons, pens, and paper clips stuck to her hands. And Inga's powers of attraction extended beyond metal objects. Witnesses actually saw books and china plates cling to her outstretched hands.

Angelique Cottin, a 14-year-old from France, had her magnetic powers for only two and a half months. During that time, compasses would spin wildly if she were close by. When she entered a room, objects near her would vibrate. If she tried to touch a piece of furniture, it would slide away from her, as if pushed.

BEAST MASTER

Vladimir Durov was an animal trainer for a Russian circus and claimed to use telepathy to train the animals. When he wanted to teach his dog, Pikki, a new trick, Durov would take Pikki's face in his hands and stare deep into the dog's eyes. He claimed to use telepathy to send orders directly into the dog's brain and the fox terrier would immediately perform the assigned trick. Skeptical scientists suspected that Durov was giving Pikki some kind of clue with his eyes, so they arranged a test. They blindfolded Durov and had him give Pikki orders just using his brain. With no eye contact or verbal instructions, Pikki did exactly what he was "told." Amazing!

ARE YOU AN X-KID?

How did these people get such strange powers? No clear

scientific x-planation x-ists. Have you ever heard the phone ring and knew who it was before you answered it? Or thought of a song, and suddenly it started playing on the radio? You could be psychic. Or maybe you can talk to animals. Go ahead—try it. Take your dog's face in your hands, stare into his eyes, and think, "Go in the kitchen and make me a ham sandwich." If he does it, you are a true beast master! (And we'll have to write about you in our next *Bathroom Reader*.)

Q: What do Albert Einstein, Tom Cruise, and Walt Disney have in common?   A: Dyslexia.

KNOCK-KNOCK

*Uncle John's best knock-knock
jokes ever. Countdown...*

Number 10
Knock-knock.
Who's there?
Oswald.
Oswald who?
Oswald my gum!

Number 9
Knock-knock.
Who's there?
Ash.
Ash who?
Gesundheit!

Number 8
Knock-knock.
Who's there?
Madame.
Madame who?
Madame foot is
caught in the
door!

Number 7
Knock-knock.
Who's there?
Duane.

Duane who?
Duane the bathtub,
I'm dwowning!

Number 6
Knock-knock.
Who's there?
Moth.
Moth who?
Moth get mythelf
a new key!

Number 5
Knock-knock.
Who's there?
Doris.
Doris who?
Doris closed, that's
why I'm knocking!

Number 4
Knock-knock.
Who's there?
Radio.
Radio who?
Radio not, here
I come!

Number 3
Knock-knock.
Who's there?
Beets.
Beets who?
Beets me—I just
forgot the joke!

Number 2
Knock-knock.
Who's there?
Dishes.
Dishes who?
Dishes the stupid-
est knock-knock
joke ever!

**And, finally,
the Number 1
best knock-knock
joke:**
Knock-knock.
Who's there?
Spell.
Spell who?
W – H – O!

TELE-VISIONARY

*What does it take for a teenage boy to come up
with one of the most important inventions
of the 20th century? Genius!*

WHIZ KID

One day back in 1921, a 14-year-old Idaho farm boy named Philo T. Farnsworth was plowing his dad's field, thinking over an idea for a new invention. Philo was crazy about electricity and spent most of his spare time reading science magazines. When he wasn't reading, he was working on his own inventions in his head.

GETTING THE PICTURE

On that particular day, Philo was trying to figure out a way to send images through the air on radio waves. He paused for a moment to look back at the field when an idea struck him: just as the field was plowed back and forth in parallel rows, why couldn't he scan an image, one line at a time, with a beam of electrons? That picture could then be sent through the air and appear on a screen one line at a time. Philo drew a sketch of an invention that would scan the pictures and showed it to his high school chemistry teacher.

Six years later, Philo T. Farnsworth actually built that invention. In 1927, at his lab in San Francisco, he sent a picture of a line from one piece of glass to

A tortoise captured by Captain Cook in the 1770s lived until 1965. It was 188 when it died.

another. "There you are!" he cried. "Electric television!"

But Farnsworth wasn't the only inventor working on television. In 1934 his patents were challenged by the media giant, Radio Corporation of America (RCA). RCA said *they*, not Farnsworth, invented television. Fortunately, Farnsworth's high school chemistry teacher, Justin Tolman, had saved the boy's original sketches from back in 1921. With those drawings, Farnsworth won the court battle against RCA and is now known as the undisputed inventor of television. In fact, the TV set that you watch today still contains about 150 parts that were invented by Philo T. Farnsworth.

NOT DONE YET

But Farnsworth didn't stop with TV. He went on to invent the first electronic microscope, an air-traffic control system, and a baby incubator. It is the television, however, for which he is best known.

*   *   *

TV IRONY

Just because he invented TV doesn't mean he let his own kids watch it.

"There is nothing on it worthwhile. We are not going to watch it in this household and I don't want it in your intellectual diet."

**—Philo T. Farnsworth,
to his son Philo, Jr.**

The average person's stomach expands from one pint (empty) to more than 10 pints (full).

MARK TWAIN SEZ

Words of wisdom from one of our favorite authors.

"If you tell the truth, you don't have to remember anything."

"It is better to deserve honors and not have them than to have them and not deserve them."

"You cannot depend on your eyes when your imagination is out of focus."

"The man who doesn't read good books has no advantage over the man who can't read them."

"Never put off until to-morrow what you can do the day after tomorrow."

"A lie can travel halfway around the world while the truth is still putting on its shoes."

"Always do right. This will gratify some people and astonish the rest."

"Be careful about reading health books. You may die of a misprint."

"When you cannot get a compliment any other way, pay yourself one."

"Keep away from people who try to belittle your ambitions. Small people always do that. The really great make you feel that you, too, can become great."

"The best way to cheer yourself up is to try to cheer someone else up."

"The human race has one really effective weapon, and that is laughter."

Blowing their money: American kids spend about $500 million on bubble gum every year.

YOUR NAME IS *WHAT?*

*Hate your name? It could be worse. Take a look
at what some famous people named their kids.*

- **Dandelion**—daughter of Rolling Stone Keith Richards

- **Dweezil** and **Moon Unit**—son and daughter of Frank Zappa, rock musician

- **Fifi Trixibelle, Pixie,** and **Peaches**—children of Bob Geldoff, organizer of the first Live Aid concert and leader of the rock group Boomtown Rats

- **Lark Song**—daughter of actress Mia Farrow and conductor André Previn

- **Zowie**—son of rock star David Bowie

- **Betty Kitten**—daughter of English TV personality Jonathan Ross

- **Sage Moon Blood**—daughter of actor Sylvester Stallone

- **Prince Michael, Prince Michael II,** and **Paris**—sons and daughter of Michael Jackson, the *King* (get it?) of Pop

- **Chastity Sun**—daughter of singers Cher and Sonny Bono

- **Sailor Lee**—daughter of model Christie Brinkley

- **Jett**—son of actor John Travolta, an amateur pilot

Fastest-growing company in Internet history: Napster.com (It went out of business).

CROCODILE HUNTER

If you watch TV, chances are you've seen Steve Irwin—the wacky Aussie who tracks down some of the world's most amazing animals to show us how they live.

WHO'S THAT IN THE BUSH?

Crikey! It's an Australian Tarzan in khaki short shorts. He rescues crocodiles, relocates dangerous snakes, and hangs out with orangutans. He's got so much energy he can barely sleep. His knowledge—and curiosity—about animals seems to be limitless. Who is he? He's Steve Irwin, the Crocodile Hunter. And he will do anything to save an animal.

How did he grow up to be a Crocodile Hunter? "You can blame my dad for that," Irwin says. "He started it. He created me. He nurtured my instincts and he caused me to be who I am, so I've followed in his footsteps." When Steve was eight, his mum and dad—the noted naturalists, Lyn and Bob Irwin—moved from Victoria to Queensland to start a reptile park.

THE NEW ZOO

For the next two years, he helped his parents catch lizards and snakes for the park. Steve's father taught him about reptiles... including how to catch crocodiles. Steve got his first go at a croc when he was nine—he caught it with his own hands.

Queensland Reptile and Fauna Park (now the

Australia Zoo) opened to the public in 1973, when Steve was 11. Not only did it feature reptiles, it also became a wildlife conservation and rehabilitation center. That's where Steve developed his passion for saving wild animals and preserving their natural habitats.

Steve later worked as a volunteer in the government's crocodile relocation program, spending years living in mosquito-infested creeks, rivers and swamps, catching troublesome crocs single-handedly.

STEVE IRWIN'S FEAR FACTOR

Even though he may not show it, the Crocodile Hunter gets scared like the rest of us. He says fear is a healthy response to dangerous situations—it keeps him from making mistakes. Does that mean he never makes mistakes? No. And his mistakes hurt. He's been bitten, scratched, poked at, attacked, and stomped on many times. But he knows that's just part of the job.

THE CROC HUNTER BECOMES A STAR

In 1990 an old friend of Steve's, television producer John Stainton, was filming a commercial for the reptile park.

Largest freshwater fish on Earth: the giant redfish of the Amazon. (It grows up to 8 feet long.)

Steve saw it as a great opportunity to show the public his passion for wildlife and a chance to demonstrate his skills with animals. That commercial inspired Steve and John to make their first documentary, *The Crocodile Hunter*, in 1992. The program was so popular that Steve and John and Steve's new bride, Terri, went on to make 10 more episodes over the next three years. Since then, Steve and Terri have filmed 50 episodes of *Crocodile Hunter* and 52 episodes of *Croc Files*.

"What happens," says Steve, "is the cameras follow me around and capture exactly what I've been doing since I was a boy. And I reckon that if I can get people excited about animals, then by crikey, it makes it a heck of a lot easier to save them!"

CROCODILE HUNTER'S DICTIONARY

If you've ever watched Steve Irwin in action, then you know he has a language of his own.

Beaut bonza mate: That's one beautiful animal, friend.

Belly full of skinks: Those snakes have been well fed.

Crikey: Holy Smokes.

Flat out like a lizard drinking: We're moving fast now.

Freshies: Freshwater crocodiles.

Good on ya: Good job!

I'm shakin' like a leaf: Whoa—that was really scary.

Muckin' about: Being really careless.

Salties: Saltwater crocodiles (much more dangerous than the freshies).

In the course of their lifetimes, crocodiles may grow up to 50 new sets of teeth.

ARACHNE

Oh what a tangled web weave when we can't keep our big mouths shut. Here is an ancient Greek myth about the price of arrogance.

Arachne (uh-rak-nee) was a young girl who was such a wonderful weaver that people came from miles around just to look at her beautiful tapestries.

"The goddess Athena must have taught you this wonderful skill," the people said. For it was Athena who taught all mortals the craft of weaving.

With a toss of her head, Arachne replied, "Athena had nothing to do with my talent. If we were to have a weaving contest, I would surely win."

Before long, Athena heard about Arachne's boasting. She disguised herself as an old woman and went to see what all the fuss was about.

Athena was very impressed by Arachne's work, but she gave the arrogant girl a warning: "Your work is lovely, my dear, but do not be so vain as to compare yourself to a goddess."

Arachne just laughed. "My work is ten times better than Athena's and given the chance, I could prove it."

With that, Athena threw off her disguise. "You shall regret those words, you silly girl. Let the contest begin."

Sound advice: To break the sound barrier, you have to fly at about 760 mph.

Athena's hands were swift and graceful. Her tapestries were beautiful. She wove scenes showing the power and might of the gods.

Arachne worked harder and faster than she'd ever worked in her life. Her tapestries were spectacular—her pictures were so realistic they almost appeared to move. But Arachne intentionally wove pictures of gods and goddesses acting stupid and foolish.

This made Athena explode with anger. "You wish to weave? Well, I grant your wish. From this day forth, you and your children, and your children's children, will weave and spin for all eternity!"

In an instant Arachne began to shrink. First her body shriveled to the size of a pea. Then her fingers turned into eight long legs. She skittered across the floor and up the wall. There she began to weave. Only this time it wasn't a tapestry—it was a web of delicate silk thread.

For Athena had turned Arachne into... a spider.

*　　　*　　　*

SPIDER FACT

Why doesn't a spider stick to its own web? It weaves special non-sticky silk strands into its web and then walks only on those.

COOL CARTOONS

*You've seen them on TV, but do you
know where they came from?*

JIMMY NEUTRON, BOY GENIUS

In the 1980s a young movie producer named John Davis drew some pictures of "Runaway Rocket Boy," a cartoon kid based on his childhood fantasies of flying into outer space. Ten years later, he purchased some sophisticated computer animation software and used it to turn his drawings into a 40-second "Rocket Boy" cartoon. He entered it in an animation festival, which is where comedy writer Steve Oedekerk (*Kung Pow: Enter the Fist*) saw it. Oedekerk then convinced Davis to make it a little longer. Their creation: a 13-minute cartoon called *The Adventures of Johnny Quasar*.

They showed it to execs at Nickelodeon, hoping the network would turn it into a series. The Nick people were so impressed that they thought it should be a TV show *and* a movie. One last thing: To avoid confusion with another fictional boy genius, Johnny Quest, they changed the name Johnny Quasar to Jimmy Neutron.

DARIA

Glenn Eichler was writing commercials for MTV when the network asked him to be a story editor for a new show called *Beavis and Butt-head*. He'd never worked in cartoons before but thought it would be fun. *B&B* creator

Mike Judge knew the show needed more than two dumb teenagers to keep viewers' interest, so Eichler came up with Daria Morgendorffer. She appeared in a few episodes of *Beavis and Butt-head.* (They taunted her with chants of "Diarrhea, diarrhea cha-cha-cha!" and she once used them as the subject of a science project.)

When *B&B* was winding down, MTV asked Eichler to create a new show around the Daria character. So he moved her to Lawndale and came up with supporting characters. The show debuted on MTV in March 1997.

CATDOG

Peter Hannan loved to draw so much that he often got in trouble in school for making little cartoons on the pages of his textbooks. When he grew up, he wrote a book called *A Few Superheroes You've Probably Never Heard Of.* One character, called CatDog Man, had two heads (one cat and one dog) and a human body. Although the book was never published, Hannan decided to combine the character with one of his favorite movies: *The Defiant Ones,* about two escaped prisoners who were chained to each other. Sound familiar?

CatDog was one of three animated shorts that Hannan was putting together for Nickelodeon. When they saw the strange two-headed, buttless beast, they told him to scrap the other two shorts and turn *CatDog* into a series. *CatDog* first aired in October 1998.

Asked how a cat and a dog joined at the butt go to the bathroom, Hannan says that he knows the secret… but he'll never tell.

Mmm…Emmys: *The Simpsons* has won 18 Emmy awards since it first aired in 1989.

FOOD FIGHTS

Sounds like leftovers in the school cafeteria, but they're stories of food that was used as weapons in real wars.

SAY CHEESE

The army of Uruguay once fought a sea battle using a new kind of cannonball: cheese. It happened in the 1840s when a dictator from Argentina tried to take over the country. He ordered his ships to blockade the port city of Montevideo, the capital. The people of Uruguay fought back from their ships in the harbor—until they ran out of ammunition. Then someone got a bright idea: raid the galleys of the ships and load their cannons with very old, hard Edam cheeses. They fired the cheese at the enemy...and won!

SPUD MISSILES

In World War II, the naval destroyer U.S.S. *O'Bannon* sank a Japanese submarine using...potatoes. It happened in the Pacific Ocean. First, the Americans shot off the sub's conning tower, stopping it from diving, but the sub was so close that they couldn't fire their big guns at it. Then, for some reason, the Japanese sailors came out on deck and the *O'Bannon* crew pelted them with potatoes. Thinking the potatoes were hand grenades, the Japanese threw their guns overboard, then panicked and submerged the sub. It sank. A plaque honoring the event was donated by Maine potato growers.

Camel's milk will not curdle.

MIND YOUR MANNERS

Uncle John believes rules are a good thing—especially when they're funny. He particularly likes this one from the 13th century: "Please refrain from falling upon the dish like a swine while eating, snorting disgustingly, and smacking the lips."

BACKGROUND

In 1530 a philosopher named Erasmus of Rotterdam wrote a book on manners called *On Civility in Children*. It was so popular that it became a bestseller of the 16th century. What was so great about it? See for yourself:

• "If you cannot swallow a piece of food, turn 'round discreetly and throw it somewhere."

• "Retain wind by compressing your belly."

• "Do not be afraid of vomiting if you must; for it is not vomiting but holding the vomit in your throat that is foul."

• "Do not move back and forth on your chair. Whoever does that gives the impression of constantly breaking or trying to break wind."

• "Turn away when spitting lest your saliva fall on someone. If anything disgusting falls on the ground, it should be trodden upon, lest it nauseate someone."

A typical fast-food milkshake contains more than 50 chemicals.

• "You should not offer your handkerchief to anyone unless it has been freshly washed. Nor is it seemly, after wiping your nose, to spread out your handkerchief and peer into it as if pearls and rubies might have fallen out of your head."

• "Some people put their hands in the dishes the moment they have sat down. Wolves do that!"

• "To lick greasy fingers or to wipe them on your coat is impolite. It is better to use the tablecloth."

*   *   *

MORE ON MANNERS

Advice from the 1880 ettiquette book
Don't: A Manual of Mistakes and Improprieties

• Don't, when you drink, elevate your glass as if you were going to stand it inverted on your nose.

• Don't devour the last morsel of food. It is not expected that your plate should be sent away cleansed by your gastronomic exertions.

• Don't say *ketch* for *catch*, or *ken* for *can*. Don't say *feller* for *fellow*, or *winder* for *window*, or *meller* for *mellow*, or *to-morrer* for *tomorrow*. Don't imagine that only ignoramuses make these mistakes.

TXT TLK

Instant messaging created a whole new shorthand language for computers and cell phone keypads. Here are some common abbreviations. (Don't write like this for school or your teacher will wonder if UROK.)

HRU ....How are you?

XLNT...Excellent!

QPSA ....Que pasa?

WENJA ....When do you

WAN2...Want to

2DAY ....Today

HCIT ....How cool is that?

WTG ....Way to go

SUM1 ....Someone

NE1 ....Anyone

BION ....Believe it or not

OIC ....Oh, I see

F2T...Free to talk

ROTFL..............Rolling on the floor, laughing

CUL8R ....See you later

The Don't in "DONT WALK" signs is misspelled—the apostrophe is missing.

SHOCKING!

The hair-raising truth about electricity.

CURRENT EVENTS

We all know electricity can be dangerous (your parents have probably been telling you that ever since you were a baby). The "Big E" gives us light and heat, and runs all of those things that make life fun, like CD players, computers, and X-Boxes. But electricity can knock you out in a second or even kill you.

WHAT HAPPENS WHEN YOU GET A SHOCK?

Electricity naturally seeks the ground. If you stick your finger in a light socket, or touch a live wire with a screwdriver, you've just given the electricity an easy path to get to the ground—through you! Water is one of the best conductors of electricity and our bodies are mostly water, so electricity jumps on us like a flea on a dog.

You don't have to be touching the ground to conduct electricity, either—you could be touching something like a ladder or a tree that, in turn, is in contact with the ground. But you have to complete the *charge-to-ground* connection. That's why birds and squirrels sitting on live power lines don't get electrocuted. Their feet aren't grounded. But if a squirrel steps off a power line onto a branch, and its feet are touching both line and tree at the same time—*Zap!* Kentucky Fried squirrel.

World speed record for a person eating live night crawlers: 94 worms...in 30 seconds.

ZAPPED!

So how does an electrical shock kill you? Like this: Our muscles are triggered to contract by electrical impulses originating from our brains. When the electrical current reaches a certain level, it makes your muscles contract. But with a sustained electric shock, nothing tells the muscle to relax, which creates a "can't let go" effect. The victim's hand muscles contract around a wire and can't release it—the current keeps the muscles contracted. Increase the current a bit and the heart muscle will be affected. A strong jolt can send the heart into *ventricular fibrillation*—beating uncontrollably out of rhythm. If this goes on too long…hasta la vista, baby.

HOW TO AVOID GETTING JOLTED

So how do the professionals avoid getting shocked?

• Electricians wear insulating shoes with rubber soles, which prevent the easy path to the ground that can result in a serious shock.

• One of the worst hazards firefighters entering a dark building face is an unseen broken power line dangling from a ceiling. What do they do? They walk with one hand extended in front of them, the back of the hand facing out. They keep the other close to their waist. Why? If they touch a wire, they'll slap *themselves*, not the wire, and avoid the "can't let go" effect.

Freshwater fish do not drink water. Saltwater fish do.

APRIL FOOLS

Have you ever wondered why people play tricks on each other every April 1? Keep wondering…because we're not going to tell you. April Fool! Here's why.

IN THE BEGINNING

Up until the mid-16th century, it was a tradition to begin the new year with a week of celebration, ending with a big party. But the calendar was different back then: years began on March 25, and the party fell on April 1. The introduction of a new calendar in 1564 made January 1 the official start of the new year. People who forgot—or didn't realize—what had happened and still showed up to celebrate on April 1 were called "April fools."

FOOLS AROUND THE WORLD

• In France, April 1 is called *Poisson d'Avril*, which means "April Fish." Children tape paper fish to their friends' backs, and when the young "fools" find out, the pranksters yell *"Poisson d'Avril!"*

• In England, tricks are only played in the morning. If a trick is played on you, you are a "noodle."

• In Scotland, you are called an "April Gowk," which is another name for a cuckoo bird.

• In Portugal, April Fool's Day is celebrated on the Sunday and Monday before Lent. Pranksters throw flour at their friends.

Sneakers were invented in 1917 (they were called Keds).

APRIL FOOL'S JOKES

Here are a few classic April Fool's jokes played by British radio and TV stations.

Pasta Farming: In 1957 the British Broadcasting Company (BBC) ran a TV documentary on "spaghetti growing" in Switzerland. Among the film's highlights: footage of Swiss farmers picking market-ready pasta from "spaghetti trees." To the BBC's astonishment, many viewers believed the phony story, including the news that Switzerland's "pasta farmers" had been able to fight off an especially destructive pest, "the spaghetti weevil."

Jumping For Pluto: In 1976 a famous British astronomer told radio audiences that since the planet Pluto would be passing behind Jupiter on April 1, the Earth's gravitational pull would decrease slightly for about 24 hours. He explained that listeners would feel the effect most if they jumped into the air at precisely 9:47 a.m. The station's switchboard was jammed with listeners calling to say that the experiment had worked.

Rainbow Radio: Also in the 1970s, a British radio station announced that it was experimenting with "color radio"—and some listeners actually reported seeing results. One complained that the experiment had affected traffic lights in his area. Another asked station managers how much longer the bright colors he saw would be streaming out of his radio.

Want some ideas for your own April Fools' jokes?
Check out "Camp Capers" on page 83.

Pretty hip: George Washington's false teeth were made of hippopotamus ivory.

ROYAL SLOBS

*Before there were bathrooms, toilets, and indoor plumbing,
where did people go? Just about anywhere they felt like
going. And that included kings and queens, who
had some pretty disgusting habits.*

K ing James I of England (reigned 1603–25)
loved hunting so much that he wouldn't leave
the saddle, even to go to the bathroom. The
king just went in his pants and had his servants clean
him up after he got home.

King Henry IV of France tried to do something about
repulsive toilet habits. In 1606 he passed a law forbid-
ding anyone to pee or poop in the corners of his palace
in Paris. His son, **The Dauphin (Louis XIII)**, issued a
similar warning—no one was allowed to pee or poop on
the floors or under stairways, either. But no one obeyed,
including the prince. The very day that he made his
announcement, he was caught peeing against the wall
of his bedroom.

King Charles II of England fled to Oxford in 1665 to
escape the plague. The people of Oxford thought the
king was a royal slob. English historian Anthony Wood
wrote about the king and his entourage in his diary:
"Although they were neat in their apparel, they were
nasty and beastly, leaving their excrement in every corner; in chimneys, studies, coalhouses, and cellars."

Two thousand years ago, Europeans washed by coating themselves with mud, then scraping it off.

King Louis XIV of France (1638–1715) thought that everything he did was royally important—including going to the bathroom. One of his favorite things to do was greet guests while seated "on the throne." Some people didn't mind doing business with the king while he was doing *his* business. They even paid to see his bare bottom, seated on the royal pot. Other people were disgusted by it, especially ambassadors from foreign lands. But that didn't stop Louis. He even announced his engagement while sitting on the pot.

*   *   *

MORE BATHROOM LORE

• In 1490 Leonardo da Vinci designed an entire sanitary city with enough toilets for everyone. Spiral staircases led to all the bathrooms. Why spiral? So there were no corners for people to pee in.

• In the 18th century, a Dr. Benjamin discovered a well in his back garden that had terrible-tasting water. Health spas were popular at the time, and the townspeople figured that anything that tasted bad had minerals in it and must be good for you. They drank the well dry only to discover it was connected to the doctor's septic tank.

• The first baron of Grimthorpe, Edmund Beckett Denison (who designed the famous clock called Big Ben in London) built a bathroom that locked a person in until they flushed the toilet.

Thirty-one percent of U.S. households have a dog. Twenty-seven percent have a cat.

SO DO ELEPHANTS

When biologists study how elephants behave in the wild, they find that they're more like humans than any other four-legged animal.

Humans Do This: When your mom has to go out somewhere, she gets a babysitter.

So Do Elephants: They live in *matriarchal* family groups, which means that the leader is a female. And other females in the group will take care of young elephants when their mothers venture off. Just like humans, elephants gain their independence when they're 18 to 20 years old. Adult females stay with the family group, but male elephants leave to form "bachelor groups," although they stay close and visit often.

Humans Do This: When you want to tell your friend something really important, you call her up.

So Do Elephants: They emit a really low sound—so low that humans can't hear it—that travels through the ground. The elephant receiving the call lifts up one leg and "listens" to the vibrations with her other three feet. They can also lay the tip of their trunks on the ground to pick up sound waves. What are they saying? According to biologists, a lot. It's not only important information about approaching storms and impending danger— it's also everyday chitchat, like, "Hey, where are you?"

That's handy: Panda bears have an immobile "thumb" that helps them grasp bamboo shoots.

Here's What Humans Do: When a close friend or relative gets back from a long trip, you have a party.

So Do Elephants: When a long-lost elephant returns to the family, a loud welcoming ceremony takes place. They spin around, flap their ears, and trumpet loudly.

Elephants like to play games, too, which isn't uncommon for mammals. But what sets elephants apart is that, like humans, both young and old ones get in on the fun. They'll play with whatever they can find—a rock, a log, even a slimy mud puddle! And just like a referee with a whistle, elephants begin a play session by trumpeting.

Here's What Humans Do: When you miss someone, do you cry? When you get mad, do you throw a tantrum?

So Do Elephants: When a baby elephant dies, the mother grieves for a long time. She holds her head low, moves very slowly, and moans a lot. Other females stay close to her, gently stroking her with their trunks.

And when an elephant gets mad, watch out! He'll take out anything in his path. Elephants are usually mild-mannered...unless they're mistreated.

Here's What Humans Do: What do you do when you're happy? You smile and laugh.

So Do Elephants: When they're happy they draw up the corners of their mouths, like a smile. And when they're really amused, they wag their head and ears back and forth and make a chortling sound...kind of like a laugh.

For more about elephants, turn to page 161.

Swimming trunks: Elephants are excellent swimmers.

CAMP CAPERS

Are you going to camp this summer? Have you been invited to a slumber party? Is your sister having a sleepover? Here are a few ways to make sure you are the life of the party. BEWARE, though: Your capers could backfire and you could become the next target.

CAPER #1: Short Sheeting the Bed

Here's a classic practical joke. Go to your friend's bed and take the top sheet and fold it in half. Then make the bed, tucking in the bottom at the halfway point on the bed. Remember to tuck it in really tight. Replace the top quilt or blanket to make the bed look normal. Try not to laugh too loud when your friend tries to stretch out her legs (or she'll know who did it).

CAPER #2: "Wetting" the Bed

Fill a small bowl with lukewarm water. Make sure it is as warm as body temperature: put a drop or two on the inside of your wrist—then you'll be able to feel if it's too cold or too hot.

Next, while your friend is sound asleep, gently take his hand and dip it into the water. Your friend will probably wet the bed, unless, of course, he wasn't really asleep…in which case, you'd better run!

Light takes 1.25 seconds to travel from the moon to Earth.

CAPER #3: Shaving Cream

This caper counts on your pal being sound asleep. Put some shaving cream in the palm of her hand. Very gently, tickle her face. Watch what happens when she tries to scratch her itch!

CAPER #4: Sardines in the Shower

Suggest that everyone play Sardines. Sardines is the hide-and-seek game where one person hides and the others look for him. As each person finds him, they squeeze into his hiding place, just like…sardines. Last one to find the group loses and is "It" for the next game. Now, when it's your turn to hide, go to the shower. Once everyone has squeezed in, turn on the water!

CAPER #5: Toilet Tricks

Tightly wrap clear plastic cling-wrap (like Saran wrap) over the toilet bowl (the bottom part) and replace the seat on top. The next person to pee will get a nasty surprise.

Warning: Don't do this if your mom or dad (or camp counselor) will be using the toilet. You could get into BIG trouble. Also, don't forget that you wrapped the toilet…or that next person could be *you*.

Another option: cover the seat with honey or syrup, or even more perfect—chunky peanut butter. Imagine going to the bathroom in the middle of the night and sitting on that. Yecch!

INSIDE THE ANTHILL

Like humans, these creepy-crawly critters live in communities and have highly developed systems for survival. They've been on Earth longer than humans have, though—in fact, about 40 million years longer. Here are some more fascinating facts about ants.

WHEN THE ANTS GO MARCHING IN

You've probably watched ants march single file across your lawn or sidewalk. Maybe they were carrying a tiny piece of bread that someone dropped on the ground. Or maybe the load was a dead beetle. Ants march in a line because they're following a trail left by other ants. The trail goes between a food source and the giant nest where the ants live.

As many as seven million ants and one queen can live in a single nest. While the queen is busy laying eggs, the worker ants hunt for food and bring it home. And they're strong: an ant can carry a load up to six times its own weight, and seven times its size. (Most humans can carry only about their own weight.)

Not only are ants strong, but they're also the hardest-working insects on the planet. There are many kinds of ants, but each one has a job and works at it night and day.

Nearly 30% of Earth is made up of oxygen.

Gardeners. Leaf cutter ants have little gardens inside their nests where they grow a type of fungus that ants like to eat. They even make their own plant food. Using their powerful mandibles (jaws), leaf cutters bite off chunks of leaves and carry them back to the nest. Then they chew and spit out the leaves to make a fertilizer for their garden.

Ranchers. While leaf cutter ants are gardeners, other ants are ranchers. Just like human ranchers keep herds of cows, rancher ants keep herds of tiny green bugs called *aphids*. These aphids make *honeydew*, which is a sweet, sticky nectar. The ants milk the aphids for their honeydew and use it for food. They also feed the aphids and protect them from being attacked (and eaten) by bigger bugs and animals.

Doctors. Believe it or not, there are even doctor ants. A scientist in Russia was watching a documentary film of ants from the Amazon. He was shocked to see three Amazonian ants extracting a splinter from the side of another ant. There was clearly one "doctor" ant who performed the surgery. The other two "nurse" ants formed a circle around the patient and doctor to protect them during the operation. The doctor ant worked carefully, and finally removed the splinter.

Slave-makers. One species of ant, sometimes called the *blood red robber ant*, builds colonies by sneaking into the nests of other ants and stealing the young ones. They carry them back to their own nests and turn them into slaves. Then they make these slave ants gather food,

Ants are *ectotherms* ("cold-blooded animals")—they can't produce their own body heat.

feed other ants, and work as maids to clean the nest.

Guards. Some ant colonies have guards to protect them from slave-makers. They block the entrance to the nest with their bodies. Many guards squirt a type of acid at their enemies. Some larger guards use their strong jaws to attack invaders.

So how do the guards know which ants are from their nest and which are strangers? By their smell. Ants have special nerve cells on their antennae that can smell odors. Each farmer, gardener, and soldier ant has its own special scent. That scent lets the others know if the ant is okay or is dangerous.

Soldiers. And speaking of dangerous, consider the most ruthless ants of all—the *driver ants* of Africa. They are some of the best killing machines in the animal kingdom. These ants move like an army, in groups of as many as 700,000 marching in rows together across the land. They'll attack and eat anything in their path—even people!

Polite guys. But don't panic—most ants are just hardworking guys (actually, most workers are females) going about their daily lives. They are very polite. When one ant wants something to eat, she gently taps her neighbor with an antenna. If there is danger, she taps a little harder as a warning.

CDs, crayons, and toothpaste all contain crude oil.

DECODING HARRY POTTER, PART I

Where does J. K. Rowling get her ideas for the characters and details in the Harry Potter books? Some of them bear an amazing resemblance to characters in Greek and Roman mythology.

The **lightning bolt.** Harry's famous scar is the symbol of Zeus, god of the sky and supreme god of the ancient Greeks.

Hermione. Hermione is the mythological daughter of King Menelaus of Sparta, Greece, and Helen of Troy—both mortals, just as Hermione's parents are Muggles.

Minerva McGonagall, one of the teachers at Hogwarts. Minerva is the Roman goddess of wisdom and of war and peace. She prefers reason to violence, except when pushed, just like Professor McGonagall.

Argus Filch. The caretaker of Hogwarts seems to know (almost) everything that goes on around the school. He is very much like the mythical Greek watchman, Argus the All-Seeing, who has 100 eyes that never close.

Fluffy, the giant three-headed guard dog. The entrance to Hades, the mythological Greek underworld, is guarded by the monster *Cerberus*. Like Fluffy, *Cerberus* is a giant three-headed dog. Also like Fluffy, he is lulled to sleep by sweet music.

J.K. Rowling is richer than the Queen of England.

X-TREME EATING

These men were leaders of our country, sports heroes, and rock stars. They were also the original plus sizes. Here's how they got to be such BIG stars.

BIG PRESIDENT: William Howard Taft
Our 27th president, "Big Bill" Taft was 6 feet tall and weighed over 300 pounds. He was so big that on his Inauguration Day, he got stuck in the bathtub…and it took six men to pull him free. Of course, Taft didn't start out big. According to some historians, a fall from a runaway carriage when he was nine left him inactive and he started eating out of boredom. Or maybe it was simply genetics. Anyway, he just could *not* stop eating! For breakfast, he would eat a dozen eggs, a pound of bacon, and stack after stack of pancakes, so when he moved into the White House in 1909, he had a special bathtub built just for him. That tub was so big it could hold four aver-age-size men…and he never got stuck again.

BIG BATTER: Babe Ruth
Babe Ruth once said, "I swing big, with everything I've got. I hit big or I miss big. I like to live as big as I can." And he ate big, too! He'd order an omelette

made with 18 eggs, plus six slices of buttered toast and three big slabs of ham on the side. For lunch he'd eat six sandwiches. His between-game snacks were chocolate ice cream and pickled eels! And Babe could swallow a full glass of soda in one swallow—ice cubes and all. Of course, he had his limits. After eating 12 hot dogs and drinking eight bottles of soda one day, he was rushed to the hospital (he survived).

BIG SINGER: Elvis Presley

The average adult man eats 2,100 calories a day. An adult Asian elephant has a normal diet of 50,000 calories a day. Before he died in 1977, Elvis—who was anything but average—was eating *between 94,000 and 100,000* calories a day! Here's the Elvis diet:

Breakfast
1 six-egg omelette
1 pound of bacon, burnt
$1/2$ pound of sausages
12 buttermilk biscuits

Lunch
2 Fool's Gold Sandwiches
Recipe: Each sandwich was made with 1 jar peanut butter, 1 jar strawberry jam, and 1 pound crisp-fried bacon on 1 French bread loaf cut in half.

Dinner
5 double hamburgers
5 deep-fried peanut butter and mashed banana sandwiches

Snacks
Pecan-crusted catfish, smoked ribs, burgers, grits and cheese, pork sandwiches, fried dill pickles, sweet potato pie, bologna cups, barbecued pizza, banana pudding, glazed donuts, and triple-layer fudge cake.

Food for thought: U.S. citizens spent $110 billion on fast food in 2000.

AMAZING COINCIDENCES

*Weird things happen all the time. Here are
a few favorites from our "freaky" file.*

KINGLY COINCIDENCE #1

King George III of England and one of his subjects, named Sam Hemming, were both born in the same town at the same moment on June 4, 1738. They both married on September 8, 1761. Each had nine sons and six daughters. Both fell ill at the same time and died on the exact same day: January 29, 1820.

KINGLY COINCIDENCE #2

King Umberto I of Italy went to Monza, Italy, on July 28, 1900. In a restaurant there, he met the owner—and thought he was looking into a mirror. The two men started talking and discovered that they were both born on the same day of the same year and in the same town: March 14, 1844, in Turin. Each was named Umberto. They each married a woman named Margherita on April 22, 1868. They each had a son named Vittorio. The two planned to meet again, the very next day, but that meeting never took place. Why? The final coincidence: they were both shot—one by accident, and the other by assassination—and both died.

First African-American to own a patent: Thomas Jennings, for a dry-cleaning process (1821).

OOPAS

OOPAs are Out-Of-Place Artifacts—objects found in places where they really don't belong. Scientists can't explain how they got there. Researchers are puzzled. Some people think OOPAs are indications that Earth has been home to some very advanced civilizations—more advanced than we are. What do you think?

1. ELECTRON TUBES IN EGYPT

In chamber 17 of the Temple of Hathor in Egypt there is a wall of engravings that look like bundles of electrical wires. According to Alfred D. Bielek, an engineer, these ancient engravings look exactly like modern engineering illustrations. In other crypts, the engravings show the electron tubes with people sitting underneath them. Were ancient people zapped with a kind of electrical radiation treatment? As far as we know, there was no electricity in ancient Egypt, so how could that be?

2. PILLAR OF IRON IN INDIA

In Delhi, India, there is a solid iron pillar that is 1,600 years old. It is over 23 feet high and weighs nearly six tons. In India, where the monsoon rains, winds, and temperatures are so extreme, any other mass of iron like this would have been reduced to rust long ago. Yet this pillar is still smooth and polished. The techniques used to make the pillar are far beyond the abilities of the people of the fifth century, when it was supposedly built. Who were the ancient metallurgists who made this pillar? What happened to their civilization?

PLANE IN EGYPT

Dr. Messiha was in the Cairo Museum of Egypt looking at bird figurines, when he found a small winged object in a box marked "Miscellaneous Items." Dr. Messiha quickly realized that this little artifact—which came from an ancient Egyptian tomb—was actually a model airplane. Of course, we all know that the ancient Egyptians didn't have airplanes, but this model had perfectly straight wings and a tail like a modern plane. Ancient Egyptians often built small models of things from their daily lives and placed them in their tombs. Could that mean that somewhere, buried deep beneath the desert sands, there are the remains of a life-size aircraft?

JET IN SOUTH AMERICA

Imagine finding a model of a high-speed aircraft over 1,000 years old. This is exactly what happened to Dr. Ivan Sanderson, in Colombia, South America. He discovered a two-inch-long "plane," probably worn on a necklace. But it looks like the Stealth bomber. It even has an insignia on the left side of the rudder, precisely where modern airliners place their ID marks. And the insignia is early Hebrew for the letter B.

A: A cat. Cats have 244—38 more than humans.

Did ancient jets fly to Colombia from the Middle East?

COMPUTER IN GREECE

Off a small island in Greece, at the bottom of the ocean, sponge divers discovered the remains of an ancient ship. The artifacts found an the ship were dated between 85 and 50 B.C. Among them was one object of great mystery: Inside a lump of corroded bronze and rotted wood were the outlines of a series of gears like you'd find in a clock. When a scientist reconstructed the machine, he discovered that it was used to calculate the annual movements of the sun and the moon. The device could show the positions of the stars in the past, present, and future... just like a computer. Ancient Greek culture was certainly advanced, but was it *that* advanced?

CRYSTAL SKULL IN MEXICO

On top of a ruined temple in an ancient Mayan city in Mexico, Dr. F. A. Mitchell-Hedges and his daughter, Anna, found an unusual artifact: a crystal sculpture of a skull. The skull, believed to be about 3,600 years old, is made from a single block of clear quartz. It is about the size of a small human skull and has almost-perfect detail. So what's the mystery? The skull was carved against the natural grain of the crystal. Carving against the axis would normally make the crystal shatter. And there are no signs that it was carved with metal tools. In fact, by all appearances, the crystal was carved using rough diamonds with repeated applications of water and silicon-crystal sand. But if that's true, then it would

Far-sighted: The Hubble Space Telescope can view newspaper print from 1 mile away.

have taken 300 years of round-the-clock carving to complete! And there weren't diamonds in Mexico at this time. So who carved it and how?

*   *   *

MOVIE TRIVIA: BEHIND THE SCENES

• In the movie *Spider-Man*, is it actor Tobey Maguire in the red-and-blue suit, a stunt man, or a computer-generated crime fighter? Says director Sam Raimi, "When Spidey is in a close-up, it's Tobey. When it's a wide shot of him swinging in, it's a stunt man. When it's Spider-Man soaring 50 stories above Manhattan, it's a computer-generated image."

• Tobey Maguire had never read a *Spider-Man* comic book before accepting the role as Peter Parker.

NOT IT!

*Uncle John likes to play tag. Do you? Here are
a few different ways to decide who's "It."*

Ibbidy, zibbidy thig
Dorey, dorey, dominig
On chee, pon chee, dom
   in non chee
Alaka, balaka, boo-boo-boo
All are out but Y-O-U.

Icka bicka soda cracker
Icka bicka boo;
Icka bicka soda cracker
Out goes Y-O-U.

Eeny meeny popsakeeny
Ah bah oobaleeny
Achy katchy Liberace
Say the magic word.
A peach, a plum,
Half a stick of chewing
   gum,
And if you want the other
   half,
This is what you say:
A man, a man
A mandiego San Diego
Hocus pocus diamondocus
Y-O-U are it.

Inka binka bottle of ink,
The cork fell off and you
   stink,
Not because you're dirty,
Not because you're clean,
Just because ya kissed a
   (boy or girl)
Behind a magazine.
And you are it.

Am stram gram,
Peekay peekay kalay
   ram
Booray booray rat ta
   tam
Am stram gram
All are out by Y-O-U.

Eeny, meeny, miny, moe,
Catch a tiger by the toe.
If he hollers make him
   pay
Fifty dollars every day.
My mother told me to
choose the very best one,
And you are not IT.

Folk remedy for hiccups: suck on a lemon.

DENTAL FLOSS

Which is older: the toothbrush or dental floss? Believe it or not, dental floss—by about 100,000 years. Grooves made by ancient dental floss have actually been found in the teeth of prehistoric human skulls.

STRING THING

Modern dental floss was officially invented by a dentist named Dr. Levi Parmly in New Orleans in 1815. He strongly recommended that his patients clean the little nooks and crevices between their teeth with a thread of silk.

In the 1940s, those silk threads were replaced by nylon threads; later, the threads were waxed. Now floss is being made with Teflon (the coating on nonstick pans) and Gore-Tex (a waterproof material used in coats). It even comes in different shapes (thread and tape) and different flavors (mint and cinnamon). And Americans must like it—they buy over three million miles of dental floss a year.

TOOTH OR DARE

But wait! Dental floss is more than just a piece of thread to clean the crevices in your teeth. It's also a chef's tool, a hiker's friend, a doctor's helper, and a prisoner's pal. Check it out:

• Chefs can use dental floss to cut dough, slice cheese, and remove biscuits that are stuck to baking sheets.

Q: What's a *genuphobe*? A: Someone who's afraid of knees.

- Hikers repair backpacks, tents, and jackets with dental floss.

- Anesthetists sometimes use dental floss to tie a breathing tube in place while the doctor operates.

- A prisoner in an Italian jail used dental floss to saw through the iron bars of his cell. How's that possible? The bars of most jails are made of a high-carbon iron which is very hard and difficult to saw through, but very brittle. In the 1970s, Italian officials were worried that terrorists with bombs might break into prisons to free their associates, so they changed all the prison bars to a softer iron which would bend, rather than break, in an explosion.

  One inmate, Vincenzo Curcio, somehow figured out that the new bars would be easier to cut and when the guards weren't looking, he sawed his way out using only dental floss.

- One prisoner saved his dental floss for months. When he had enough of it, he braided it into a rope and used it to climb the prison walls... and escape.

MASTERS OF DISGUISE

Here's a little mystery for you to solve. All the clues you need are in the story. It's easy—just use logic and reason (or you can cheat and look up the answer on page 283).

A FRIENDLY BOAST

Uncle John, his sidekick, J. Porter Newman, and their friend Mr. Ollie Tidball received invitations to the annual Bathroom Readers' Institute Costume Ball. They were thrilled. Each was certain that his costume would be better than the others.

"I am the Master of Disguise," said Uncle John. "When I'm in costume, no one will be able to guess my true identity."

"Ha!" replied J. Porter Newman. "My costume will be so good, my own mother won't recognize me. For I am the *true* Master of Disguise."

Mr. Tidball was quiet but firm: "Sorry to disagree, but *my* costume will be the best. Nary a soul will be able to guess who I am—you see, I am the Master."

THE CHALLENGE

Elbow Room, Uncle John's talking dog, had been listening to them all boast and growled, "Grrrrr-racious. I bet I'll be able to guess who you are within two minutes—without sniffing you."

In your lifetime, you'll spend the same amount of time eating as you do blinking.

"Flying flushes!" cried Uncle John. "Is that a challenge?"

"Yep!" yipped Elbow Room.

WHO'S WHO?

On the night of the costume ball, Elbow Room waited in the great hall of the Bathroom Readers' Institute with his friend Hairball, the coughing cat.

The three Masters of Disguise—a ferocious-looking gorilla, a purple Teletubby, and a knight in shining armor—walked in. Hairball carefully licked one paw and purred, "I recognize them. The gorilla is Uncle John, the knight is Tidball, and the Teletubby is Newman."

Jeffrey, the butler, who had helped the men into their costumes and knew which was which, declared, "Sorry! All wrong!" Humiliated, Hairball promptly left the hall.

Now it was up to Elbow Room. He didn't like to admit it, but the disguises were good—maybe too good.

Two minutes were almost up, when the gorilla leaned over to the man beside him and whispered, "Looks like we fooled them, eh, Tidball?"

"Hush!" hissed the other man. "You'll give us away!"

Elbow Room immediately howled, "I've got it! I've flushed you out! I know who's who!"

Do you know? Turn to page 283 to find out.

The word purple comes from *purpura*, the Latin name of a purple shellfish used to make dye.

STAR POWER

Imagine starting the new school year by demanding a desk with a view, three six-packs of soda, a bowl of purple jelly beans, and a clean pair of socks. Now imagine your new teacher saying, "Of course! Is there anything else?"

SPOILED ROTTEN

Celebrities have contracts with a special section called a *rider*. The rider lists all the extra things the celebrity wants before he or she will go to work. And some stars want and need some *very* odd things. Here are a few examples:

Shania Twain
- Mori-Nu silken-style soft tofu
- Four bananas and three papayas
- Organic cheese popcorn

(*Note:* She travels with a bomb-sniffing patrol dog.)

Marilyn Manson
- A box filled with fresh kitty litter (in case the bathrooms are out of order)

Moby
- Ten pairs of white cotton crew socks
- Ten pairs of cotton boxer shorts

Backstreet Boys
- Twenty-four peanut butter and jelly sandwiches
- Hot coffee, tea, and a gallon of milk
- Absolutely *no* candy, chips, chocolate, or junk food

Driving with the windows up can increase gas mileage by as much as 10%.

Christina Aguilera

• Six-pack of Coke (no Pepsi, no diet)

• Carnation Instant Breakfast, malt flavor

• Organic whole milk and Oreo cookies

• Liter of vanilla soy milk (must not contain canola oil, barley, oats, or malt of any kind)

• Small bottle of Flintstones vitamins

• Mozzarella soy cheese

• Tray of organic veggies (must include jicama)

Leonardo DiCaprio (on the set of the movie *Gangs of New York*)

• New clothes delivered daily—the ones worn the day before were to be thrown out.

Michael Jackson

• Never refer to him as a "mega-star." He is now a "giga-star."

Ricky Martin

• Orange-colored lighting (to highlight his tan)

Kid Rock

• A new bag of Hanes boxer shorts at every tour stop. (He refuses to wear the same pair twice.)

Britney Spears

• Seven dressing rooms

• Pop Tarts, Cap'n Crunch, Fruit Loops, and Cool Ranch Doritos

• Mocha latte from her favorite Los Angeles coffee shop. If she's not in L.A., the promoters must have it flown in to her.

• The promoter has to pay her $5,000 everytime she gets a phone call she doesn't want.

Mariah Carey

• All posters of pop-star rivals must be removed, especially those of Christina Aguilera.

A DEVOTED FRIEND

"A dog is the only thing on this Earth that loves you more than he loves himself." —Anonymous

GREYFRIARS BOBBY

One of the most loyal dogs who ever lived was a Skye Terrier named Bobby. As a puppy, he was adopted by an elderly Scottish shepherd named "Old Jock" Gray. Old Jock died in 1858, and for the next 14 years, Bobby guarded his master's grave at the Greyfriars churchyard, day and night. He howled when concerned citizens tried to keep him indoors in bad weather...until they let him out to return to the grave.

He would leave it for a short time each day, only to go to the same restaurant where his master used to go. According to legend, the restaurant owner would give him a bone and then Bobby would carry it away, back to the grave. The citizens of Edinburgh built a shelter to shield Bobby from the cold winters, and when he died in 1872, he was buried beside Old Jock. A statue and fountain of Bobby still stands there with this inscription: *Let his loyalty and devotion be a lesson to us all.*

Q: Why was the first space shuttle named *Enterprise*? A: *Star Trek* fans lobbied for it.

ASK DR. FUTURE

Who is Dr. Future? A mysterious visitor from the world of Tomorrow. He's here to tell us some of the things scientists are doing right now to help save the environment for the future.

UNCLE JOHN: Dr. Future, we keep hearing that we're destroying our environment. Will we ever be able to fix it?

DR. FUTURE: Not to worry, Johnny Boy. In my time the air is clean, the water is pure, and pollution is all but gone!

UNCLE JOHN: But how? Americans throw away more than 35 billion pounds of plastic garbage every year. Surely our landfills are running out of room!

DR. FUTURE: Settle down, John...and don't call me Shirley. Your scientists are already trying to fix the problem. Soon all sorts of plastic products will come from landfills: furniture, appliances, even clothes. Recycled plastic grocery bags are already being turned into jackets that look and feel just like leather. And you know those little Styrofoam peanuts you use for packing boxes? They're being recycled into insulation to put inside the jackets.

UNCLE JOHN: But what about all the other things that get thrown away?

The whites of your eyes are called the sclera.

DR. FUTURE: As time goes on, my friend, fewer and fewer products will be made that have to be thrown away. Your time is already seeing a new kind of fabric that's strong enough to carry heavy groceries, but gentle enough to use as a hospital gown. Best of all, it also dissolves in hot water, so when you're done with it, it goes into the sink—not in the landfill.

UNCLE JOHN: But what about the oceans? Oil spills create poisonous slicks that spread for miles. They kill every living thing in their paths and are almost impossible to clean up.

DR. FUTURE: Impossible in your time, perhaps. But in the near future those nasty spills will be cleaned up with a giant, super-absorbent cloth that can suck up more than five times its weight in oil. And the fabric is recyclable—even after a messy cleanup.

UNCLE JOHN: Speaking of messy cleanups, my little nephew goes through five disposable diapers a day. It can take anywhere from several months to several years for a plastic diaper to break down in a landfill. What's being done about that?

DR. FUTURE: Well, you need to add something to those diapers—besides poop—to break them down.

UNCLE JOHN: What?

DR. FUTURE: Would you believe dead fish? It's true. In

the future, we've solved the disposable diaper problem by solving another problem: Commercial fishermen end up with a lot of dead fish in their nets that they don't want. It's called the by-catch. These smelly carcasses used to be thrown back into the ocean—where they would end up polluting tidal basins and beaches.

But not anymore. In my time, the inside of disposable diapers are coated with a gel made from the by-catch. The gel is pure protein, doesn't smell at all like dead fish, and absorbs up to 600 times its own weight. Bacteria and fungi eat it up. Soon, it will take only 28 days in a landfill for the fishlined diaper to degrade.

UNCLE JOHN: It seems like the possibilities for recycling are endless.

DR. FUTURE: You love to state the obvious, don't you? Yes, my precious publisher of popular privvy-reading. People all over the world are constantly figuring out new and ingenious ways to conserve energy and resources. You just need to do what you can to help today and keep looking toward the future.

UNCLE JOHN: Wonderful! So…who will win next year's Super Bowl?

DR. FUTURE: Well, gotta go! See ya on my next trip to the past!

Why don't they call it a sea *pony?* An adult dwarf sea horse is less than 2 inches long.

FUNNY LADIES

One-liners from some of our favorite comedians.

"When I was a kid, I only had two friends. They were imaginary, and they would only play with each other."
—**Rita Rudner**

"You have to stay in shape. My grandmother started walking five miles a day when she was 60. Now she's 97 and we have no idea where she is."
—**Ellen DeGeneres**

"Statistics say that one out of four Americans suffer from mental illness. Think of your three best friends. If they're okay, then it's you."
—**Rita Mae Brown**

"I come from a family where gravy is considered a beverage."
—**Erma Bombeck**

"My parents used to stuff me with candy. M&M's, jujubes, SweeTARTS. I don't think they wanted a child, I think they wanted a piñata."
—**Wendy Leibman**

"When I was born I was so surprised, I didn't talk for a year and a half."
—**Gracie Allen**

"My mother told me I would never amount to anything because I procrastinate. I said, 'Just wait.'"
—**Judy Tenuta**

"Why does Sea World have a seafood restaurant? Halfway through my fishburger, I realized *'Oh my God, I could be eating a slow learner.'*"
—**Lynda Montgomery**

Babies blink about once a minute; adults blink about once every five seconds.

KIDS ON STRIKE!

This little-known story from American history proves that kids can stand up for their rights—and win— when they're being treated unfairly.

EXTRA! EXTRA! READ ALL ABOUT IT! Back in the 1890s, there were about 10,000 homeless children living on the streets of New York City. At night, they slept in doorways, in alleys, under stairways, or anywhere else they could find shelter. In the daytime, they tried to find work. Many of them became *newsies*, kids who sold newspapers on the streets. They bought papers from the newspaper companies for one price and then sold them for a little bit more.

And the more they sold, the more they earned. So they stood on street corners and yelled out the headlines, urging people to buy their papers. On a good day, a newsie would make 30 cents, barely enough for food and not enough for clothing or shelter.

MILLIONAIRES WANT MORE!

William Randolph Hearst and Joseph Pulitzer were two of the richest and most powerful men in America. Each one owned a giant newspaper in New York City. They counted on the newsies to hit the streets and sell their papers. In early July 1899, sales were slow, so these two millionaires decided to make up for it by charging the newsies more money for their papers. They figured the

---

Surf's down: The Aral Sea in central Asia has decreased 80% in volume since 1960.

newsies couldn't do anything about it because, after all, they were just kids. They were wrong.

STRIKE!

Led by three boys called Kid Blink (he was blind in one eye), Racetrack Higgins, and Boots McAleenan, hundreds of newsies met in City Hall Park on July 18, 1899, and formed a union. Kid Blink took charge and spoke to the other kids:

> "Friends and fellow workers, this is a time which tries the hearts of men. This is the time when we've got to stick together like glue. We know what we wants and we'll get it, even if we is blind!"

The newsies refused to sell Hearst's *New York Journal* or Pulitzer's *New York World* until their buying price went back down.

HELP THE NEWSBOYS!

The newsies not only refused to sell the *Journal* or the *World*, they also were determined to make sure nobody *else* could, either.

• Sometimes hundreds of kids would surround the paper delivery wagons and threaten to beat up the drivers.

• Mobs of kids yanked papers out of people's hands and tore them up.

• Angry boys hurled rocks at the men Hearst and Pulitzer had hired to replace them. (And even though the millionaires demanded protection, the newsies were fast and could usually outrun the cops.)

Other newspapers gleefully made heroes of the striking kids, giving them front-page coverage. The public supported their cause and refused to buy Hearst's and Pulitzer's papers.

SPREAD THE WORD!

The newsies' strike quickly spread to Connecticut, New Jersey, and Massachusetts. The *World* and *Journal* were starting to lose money, but Hearst and Pulitzer still wouldn't budge. Another rally was organized in lower Manhattan, and this time 5,000 kids showed up. When Kid Blink leaped onto the speaker's platform, the cheers were deafening. Kid raised his hands for silence and then scratched his head, as if he were puzzled.

"I'm trying to figure out how ten cents on a hundred papers can mean more to a millionaire than it does to us newsboys. And I can't see it."

The newsies vowed to keep striking until Hearst and Pulitzer begged them to stop. "It's great," Kid Blink told a newspaper reporter. "They can't beat us. Me noble men is all loyal, and with such as these to oppose their nefarious schemes how can those blokes hope to win?"

VICTORY!

When sales dropped by two-thirds, both Hearst and Pulitzer finally gave up. In early August, they offered the newsies a deal that kept the prices the same, and even let the newsies return any unsold papers and get their money back. The newsies took the deal…and in the end, they made even more money than before.

In the 15th and 16th centuries, Europeans called bananas "Indian figs."

LUCKY ACCIDENTS

Have you ever thought you messed something up, only to discover that the result turned out to be totally cool? Believe it or not, that's how a lot of everyday products first came into the world. Here are a few examples.

SILLY PUTTY

Scientists were trying to make synthetic rubber and accidentally ended up with this bouncy, stretchy stuff. It seemed worthless. How could it be used?

Here's the lucky part: A toy salesman happened to see some adults playing with it and realized that it would make a great toy. With only $147, he started a company to sell the goo and named it Silly Putty. Today the factory uses a cement mixer to mix the ingredients and a taffy machine to slice it into little portions. More than three million Silly Putty eggs are sold each year.

SAFETY GLASS

In 1903 Edouard Benedictus, a French chemist, accidentally dropped a glass container on the floor. He expected the floor to be covered with little bits of glass. Instead he found that the broken pieces were held together against a thin film of liquid plastic, which had been inside the container. Benedictus was inspired. From this lucky accident, he invented a glass that, if it breaks, does not shatter. It's called *safety glass* and it's used primarily for automobile windows.

Plan(t) ahead: It takes 3 years for asparagus to grow big enough to eat.

PINK BUBBLE GUM

In 1928 a 23-year-old employee of the Fleer Company invented a bubble gum that wouldn't stick to people's faces. As he was mixing up the first batch, he realized he'd forgotten to put any color in the gum. The next day, he made a second batch. This time he remembered to color it. What color should he make it? He looked around the lab. The only color dye he could find was…pink, so that's what he used. The color stuck. And that's why most of the bubble gum sold today is pink.

STICK MATCHES

In 1827 an English pharmacist named John Walker was trying to create a new explosive. He was mixing some chemicals with a wooden stick when he noticed a tear-shaped glob had dried on the end of the stick. Trying to clean it off, he scraped the stick across his stone floor and, all of a sudden, the tip burst into flame. Walker had accidentally invented the world's first friction match.

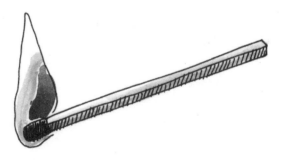

Shh! The formula for Play-Doh is top secret—Playskool keeps it under lock and key.

HAVE AN ICE DAY

*Hockey fans are loud, loyal, and...weird. Here
are some of the odd things they've done to show their
appreciation—or lack of appreciation—for the game.*

FLYING OCTOPI

It all began on April 15, 1952. During the
Detroit Red Wings' Stanley Cup run they
won an unprecedented eight straight
games. Two local fans, Pete and Jerry
Cusimano, came up with an
unusual way of celebrating the
feat—with an octopus. Why an
octopus? Each arm of the octopus
represented one win in the playoffs. In
the stands, the proud Cusimano brothers
stood up and hurled an octopus onto the ice—during
the game! Ever since then, fans of the Red Wings have
chucked octopi onto the ice after every big win.

I SMELL A RAT

It was 1995, the Year of the Rat in Chinese astrology.
On October 8 at approximately 6:30 p.m. a rat charged
into the Florida Panthers locker room. All of the hockey
players were screaming and scrambling to get out of the
way, except one—Scott Mallanby. When the rat zeroed
in on him, Mallanby one-timed it with a slap of his
stick, slamming it against the locker-room wall.

Octopus blood is pale blue.

Later that night, Mallanby scored two goals in a 4–3 win. John Vanbiesbrouck dubbed it the "rat trick." Word got out, and two games later, on October 13, two rubber rats were tossed onto the ice after a Panther goal. Sixteen rubber rats were thrown on the ice during the next game. The game after that: 50 rats. By the time the playoffs began, fans were pelting the ice with so many rats that the opposition goalie had to hide in the net.

Because the games were delayed for so long in order to remove the rats, the National Hockey League created an official rule banning the tossing of rubber rats onto the ice.

DUCK—IT'S A PUCK!

November 14, 2001, is a night Pittsburgh Penguin fans will never forget. Each fan entering the Mellon Arena was given a regulation-size, fully weighted, commemorative hockey puck to celebrate the three most recent inductees into the Penguins Hall of Fame. Everything was fine until the third period, when Penguin Alexei Kovalev scored three goals (which is known as a *hat trick*). Fans started cheering and throwing their hats onto the ice (another hockey tradition).

When they ran out of hats, they started chucking the only things left in their hands: pucks. The hockey players—who typically aren't afraid of anything—were ducking and cowering near the glass and under benches. Luckily only one player—Penguins forward Dan La Couture—was hurt. "You expect bumps and bruises on the ice," he said. "But certainly not from the stands."

Sir Isaac Newton invented the cat door.

THE DEVIL'S DOZEN

Are you afraid of the number 13, also known as the "devil's dozen"? Then you have triskaidekaphobia. *Don't worry, you're not alone. The number 13 has been considered unlucky almost as far back as people can remember.*

D**ID YOU KNOW?**
- Many hotels have no room number 13.
- Hospitals often have no room 13.
- Many cities don't have a 13th St.

- The lotteries in France, Italy, and many other countries never sell tickets with the number 13.

- Many athletes refuse to wear 13 on their jerseys.

- 13 is the death card in a tarot deck.

- There are 13 witches in a coven.

- Airlines skip the 13th row of seating.

13 People = Bad Luck for Hindus

Hindus have long believed that it is unlucky for 13 people to gather anywhere.

13 at the Last Supper = Bad Luck for Christians

For Christians, the number 13 also brings bad luck. The superstition stems from the Last Supper, where Judas Iscariot became the 13th guest to sit at the table. Judas later betrayed Jesus, leading to his crucifixion. To

---

Just like teenagers: House cats spend about 70% of their day sleeping and 15% grooming.

this day, it is considered very bad luck for 13 people to sit down for dinner together. It is believed that one of the dinner guests will die within the year.

XIII = Bad Luck for Romans

Ancient Romans also believed the number 13 was bad luck. They associated it with death and misfortune. Why? There were 12 months in a year and 12 hours in a day (according to the Roman clock), so 13 was seen as a violation of the natural cycle.

Unlucky *Apollo 13*

Apollo 13's mission lifted off at 13 minutes past the 13th hour on 4/11/70 (4 + 1 + 1 + 7 + 0 = 13) from Pad #39 (39 = 3 x 13). On April 13, an oxygen tank exploded, almost killing the three astronauts inside.

Friggatriskaidekaphobia (Fear of Friday the 13th)

Why is Friday so feared? Some people say it's because Adam and Eve were thrown out of Eden on a Friday. Others say it's because Noah's flood started on a Friday. Whatever the reason, fear of Friday the 13th is one of the most widespread superstitions of all. Some people won't go to work on that day. Others won't eat in restaurants or drive. Many wouldn't think of setting a wedding on that date. But too bad for those people— the 13th is more likely to fall on a Friday than on any other day of the week.

EARTHQUAKE!

Earthquakes are among the most destructive forces on Earth because they can cause the most damage in the least amount of time. Even more than your brother.

FEELING SHAKY?

Don't get up now, but there's a 100% chance that an earthquake is going to register somewhere in the world while you're reading this page. That's because there are about a million earthquakes per year—about one every 30 seconds. You probably won't even feel it, though: humans feel *only* about 60,000 earthquakes a year—about one every 10 minutes somewhere on the planet. And most of these don't do any damage at all.

The average earthquake lasts less than a second, but the most damaging ones, called *great earthquakes,* can last for as long as several minutes. Fortunately, there's only about one of these a year.

TIDAL WAVE!

Earthquakes can also cause huge high-speed waves known as *tsunamis* (soo-NAM-mee), or *tidal waves.* (Volcanic eruptions can also cause these.)

When an earthquake occurs somewhere beneath the ocean, the ocean floor shifts, creating a huge ripple in the water. This ripple spreads out in a circle, at speeds up to 600 miles per hour. Because the ocean is so deep, the ripple is barely noticeable…at first. But as the ripple nears the shallows and the shore, a wall of water is pushed upward, creating a devastating tsunami.

Because they appear with hardly any warning, tsunamis have wreaked havoc on coastal communities for centuries. Today they can be detected by satellites, which gives local authorities time to evacuate people in danger. But just in case you're alone on a secluded beach, here's nature's warning sign: If the ocean's water level drops drastically in a very short period of time, get to high ground as fast as you can. A tsunami is coming!

THE BIG ONE OF '64

Many people think the earthquake capital of the U.S. is California, but it's actually Alaska. More quakes occur there per year than in the rest of the country combined.

America's strongest and largest recorded earthquake rocked the southwest coast of Alaska on March 27, 1964. Earthquake waves swept through the land at more than 7,000 miles per hour. Buildings, bridges, and roads crumbled. Railroad tracks bobbed up and down, hurling trains into the air. In some areas, the earth dropped 35 feet, in others it rose 50 feet. Even thousands of miles away, the ground was affected—NASA noted that it lifted 2 to 4 inches in Florida and in Texas.

Tsunamis caused by the great Alaskan quake swamped at least 68 fishing boats, and crashed into the shores of Canada and Hawaii. Amazingly, in all this devastation, only about 115 people died. The reason? Few people lived in Alaska in 1964.

There are more than 600 active volcanoes on Earth. At least 80 of them are in the ocean.

HAUNTED SUMMER

The original Frankenstein's monster wasn't from a movie or a comic book, it was a character created by a teenage author named Mary Shelley...more than 180 years ago.

I T WAS A DARK AND STORMY NIGHT
Lightning flashed outside the huge mansion on Lake Geneva as rain pelted the windows like thousands of hands hammering to get in. The four friends at Lord Byron's manor moved closer to the fireplace. Was there nothing they could do to stop this endless rain?

It was the summer of 1816. The poet Percy Bysshe Shelley and his fiancée, 19-year-old Mary Wollstonecraft, were on holiday in Switzerland. But they hadn't seen the sun since their arrival. They were going stir-crazy.

A NOVEL IDEA

On this particular night, Mary and Percy were visiting their neighbor, 28-year-old Lord Byron and his friend, Dr. Polidori. As the storm raged outside, they entertained each other by reading ghost stories aloud.

Then Byron closed his book, and as lightning lit the room, he whispered, "I have an idea. We shall each write a ghost story." They agreed to retire to their rooms and see who could write the most frightening story.

The storm raged on. They toiled away, but it was harder than they thought. Because they were all poets, writing stories of horror did not come naturally to them.

Q: What do you call someone who studies caves? A: A *speleologist.*

That night, Mary tossed and turned in her sleep. She was determined to come up with the best story—one which "would speak to the mysterious fears of our nature and awaken thrilling horror." Yet she couldn't come up with anything.

The next morning, the group shared their results. Byron had the start of a story about a man who returns from the dead. Percy had written a story that they all agreed was forgettable. Dr. Polidori's tale was a genuine spine-tingler called "The Vampyre." The main character, Lord Ruthven, was "a jaded, charismatic nobleman who must feed upon the blood of the living in order to continue his unnatural existence." (Years later, Polidori's character was adapted into a play, a novel, and then a movie: *Dracula*.)

Mary was the only one who hadn't come up with anything. Days passed. Every morning, her companions asked, "Have you thought of a story?" And each morning, she "was forced to reply with a mortifying negative."

A FLASH OF INSPIRATION

One evening Mary sat by the fireplace, listening to her husband and Lord Byron talk about the possibility of reanimating a corpse with electricity, giving it what they called "vital warmth." The discussion came to an end well after midnight, and Percy went off to bed. But Mary couldn't sleep.

"When I placed my head upon the pillow," she recalled, "I did not sleep, nor could I think." Her

imagination led her into a dream world filled with pictures of a pale young man kneeling beside a strange device he had built. The hideous shape of a dead body was stretched out on an operating table before him. Then she saw the corpse, under the power of some strange engine, jerk and shudder back to life. This "horrid thing" then stood up and looked at his creator with "yellow, watery eyes."

Mary sat up in terror. She looked around the room for something to reassure her that it was only a dream, but she couldn't shake the image of the hideous creature. That was when she realized her vision was, in

Every known living thing has a two-part Latin name. Yours is *Homo sapiens* ("wise man").

fact, the story she'd been searching for.

"I have found it!" she thought. "What terrified me will terrify others; and I need only describe the specter which haunted my midnight pillow." The next day, Mary announced to the group that she had finally thought of a story. It was called *Frankenstein*.

THE HORROR CONTINUES

The first version was just a short story, but after they were married, Percy encouraged Mary to develop it further, and she eventually turned it into a novel. It was published anonymously in three parts in 1818.

"Mary," notes one modern critic, "did not think it important enough to sign her name to the book. And since her husband wrote the book's preface, people assumed he had written the rest of the book as well.... It was not until a later edition of *Frankenstein* that the book was revealed as the work of a young girl."

*   *   *

CREATURE FEATURES

More than 60 movies have been based on Mary Shelley's creation. Here are a few of the odder titles:

• *Frankenstein Meets the Space Monster* (1965)

• *Jesse James Meets Frankenstein's Daughter* (1965)

• *I Was a Teenage Frankenstein* (1957)

• *Frankenstein General Hospital* 1988)

• *Frankenstein's Castle of Freaks* (1973)

• *Frankenstein's Great-Aunt Tillie* (1983)

Pikachu is Japanese for "electric mouse."

WHERE'S THE JOHN?

Uncle John used to be a little sensitive about bathrooms being called johns. *But he got over it. Turns out that there are a lot of other names for the bathroom. Here are a few of our favorites.*

A JOHN BY ANY OTHER NAME...

The Restroom
The Loo
The WC
The Head
The Potty

The Comfort
Station
The Water Closet
The Latrine
The Little Boys'
(or Girls') Room

The Can
The Throne
The Biffy
The Necessary
The Lav

NAMES ON PUBLIC RESTROOM DOORS:

Men and
Women
Pointers and
Setters
Guys and Dolls
Johns and Janes

Jacks and Jills
Knights and
Dames
Combs and
Brushes
Lads and Lassies

His and Hers
Bucks and Does
Kane and
Wahini (it's
Hawaiian)
Buoys and Gulls

OTHER WAYS OF SAYING YOU HAVE TO GO
I have to...

"shake a leaf."

"see a man about
a horse."

"powder my nose."

"water the garden."

"strain the potatoes."

"catch a mouse."

"drop the kids
off in the pool."

In the U.S., one pound of potato chips costs 200 times more than one pound of potatoes.

A SLICE OF LIFE

Here is Uncle John's history of one of
the best foods ever invented—pizza.

PIE'S THE LIMIT

The ancient Greeks were the most accomplished bakers of the ancient world. They made a variety of breads topped with spices, herbs, and vegetables. These concoctions—a kind of "edible plate"—were the first pizzas. How did pizza become Italian? The Greeks occupied part of Italy for six centuries, and one of the things they brought with them was pizza.

Early pizzas featured cheese, herbs, vegetables, and fish or meat—but no tomatoes. Tomatoes, a New World food, didn't reach Italy until the mid-1500s and didn't become popular until the 1800s because some people believed they were poisonous.

CREATING THE CLASSIC PIZZA

In 1889 King Umberto and Queen Margherita of Italy visited Naples and wanted to sample the most popular local food, which was pizza. They sent word to Chef Raffaele Esposito, and he brought them a local favorite, *pizza alla mozzarella* (toppings: tomato, basil, and mozzarella cheese).

Why he chose those particular ingredients is unknown. Some historians say he wanted to make a pizza in the colors of the Italian flag—red, white, and green. But whatever the reason, the queen loved it. She sent him a thank-you note and he returned the compliment by dedicating the *pizza alla mozzarella* to her and renaming it *Pizza Margherita* in her honor. It is considered *the* classic by pizza chefs and is still called Pizza Margherita. One more thing makes that particular pizza a classic: it's the first-known pizza delivery.

PIZZA IN THE NEW WORLD

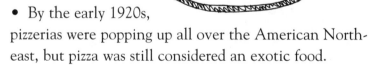

• The first American pizzeria was opened in New York's Little Italy in 1905.

• By the early 1920s, pizzerias were popping up all over the American Northeast, but pizza was still considered an exotic food.

• American soldiers returning from Italy after World War II spread pizza's popularity throughout the United States. But it wasn't until the 1960s that it became a fad. One possible reason: In the 1961 film *Splendor in the Grass*, Warren Beatty asks a waitress, "Hey, what is pizza?" Before that, most Americans had never heard of it.

• Pepperoni is the most popular pizza topping nationwide; anchovies are the least favorite.

• Today Americans eat more than 30 million slices of pizza a day—or 350 slices a second—and spend $25 billion a year on it.

Alicia Silverstone began her acting career in a Domino's Pizza commercial.

COOKING WITH UNCLE JOHN

You'll love this recipe. We brought it all the way from Transylvania. (Don't fang us now—you can fang us later.)

VANT A DRINK?

FAKE BLOOD
Ingredients:
- 2 tablespoons light corn syrup
- 1 tablespoon water
- 2 to 4 drops red food coloring
- 3 pinches cornstarch
- 2 pinches cocoa

Recipe: Place the corn syrup into a cup and add the spoonful of water. Stir with a toothpick. Then add the drops of red food coloring and stir it again. Pour the mixture into a plastic bag and add the pinches of cornstarch and cocoa. Seal the bag and squish it all together. Voilà! You've made blood fit for a vampire!

Want to pretend you're Dracula? Drip some of your new fake blood out of the corner of your mouth. Want to fake out your mom? Drip some of it under your nostril and tell her your nose is bleeding. *Warning:* This blood, like real blood, will stain clothes and carpeting. So it's best to use it outside.

OLD R.I.P.

If you're ever in Eastland, Texas, be sure to visit the Eastland County Courthouse. It is the final resting place of Old Rip, the most famous horned lizard in the world.

LEAPIN' LIZARDS

Old Rip's story begins back in 1897. In those days, people used to say a horned lizard could live for 100 years without food or water. A local kid named Will Woods wanted to know if that was true.

About that time, the town was building a new courthouse. During the ceremony for the laying of the cornerstone, Justice of the Peace Ernest Woods (Will's dad) placed a Bible, a newspaper, and a few other mementos into the cornerstone. Then, as a sort of joke, Mr. Woods dropped in a horned lizard that Will had found out in the desert. The stone was sealed and the courthouse built on top of it.

A VERY LONG NAP

Thirty-one years went by. Then, in 1928, the townspeople decided they needed a new courthouse. Just as they were getting ready to tear the old building down, some people remembered the horned lizard sealed into it three decades before. Could the lizard still be alive?

On the day of the demolition, 3,000 people showed up to watch the opening of the horned lizard's tomb. He was still there, but he was as flat as a piece of cardboard and covered in dust.

IT'S ALI-I-I-I-VE

The county judge grabbed the lifeless creature by the leg and held him high in the air for all to see. To the crowd's astonishment, the lizard's other leg suddenly quivered. Then the lizard's body inflated as it took a big gulp of air. That was its first breath of fresh air in 31 years!

The average life span of a horned lizard is about seven years. But somehow this one had gone into hibernation. People quickly named the lizard "Old Rip," after the legendary Rip Van Winkle, the man who slept for 20 years.

DEAD AGAIN

Old Rip instantly became famous. People wanted to see this creature that had managed to live without food or water for 31 years. Old Rip went on tour. He even visited the White House and met President Coolidge.

Old Rip lived for another year. When he died, the town had him stuffed and put into a little casket lined with velvet.

And there he remained until 1962, when Governor John Connally stopped in Eastland on his reelection campaign tour. Unfortunately, at one rally, Governor Connally held Old Rip up in the air for the crowd to see...and dropped him, snapping off one of Rip's legs.

Today, Old Rip, minus one leg, lies in his casket in a glass case in the courthouse lobby. If you are ever in Eastland, stop by and say, "Howdy, Old Rip!"

Peeee-eeew! *Osphresiophobia* is the fear of body odors.

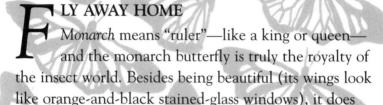

ROYAL INSECT

Here's an amazing fact from nature, a
mystery that scientists can't explain.

FLY AWAY HOME

Monarch means "ruler"—like a king or queen—
and the monarch butterfly is truly the royalty of
the insect world. Besides being beautiful (its wings look
like orange-and-black stained-glass windows), it does
something truly remarkable.

Like all butterflies, it develops from an egg, to a
caterpillar, to a chrysalis, and finally into a butterfly.
Then it lays its eggs. And then it migrates. What's so
remarkable about that?

• Every year, *all* the monarchs in the cold regions of
the United States and Canada—nearly 100 million of
them—fly south to Mexico, Florida, and California.

• They fly at speeds up to 12 mph, traveling as far as
50 miles a day! A migrating monarch may cover 2,000
miles on this one-way journey.

• They're in constant danger of being struck by cars,
battered by storms, and eaten by predators, such as
birds, mice, wasps, and spiders. But still they fly on.

• Here's the most remarkable part: generation after
generation of monarchs not only migrate to the same
spot their ancestors flew to—they often go to the exact
same tree!

In 1952 Albert Einstein was offered the presidency of Israel. He declined.

LET THERE BE LIGHTS

Mysterious lights have confused, frightened, and entertained people for thousands of years. Some we now understand. Others remain a mystery.

FIREFLIES

You're probably familiar with the little lights that flicker on and off in our backyards on summer nights: fireflies. But what makes them glow? *Bioluminescence.* This is the scientific word that describes the emission of light when certain living things meet up with oxygen. Have you ever seen the ocean and noticed that the waves seem to glow at night? That's caused by the bioluminescence of tiny creatures that live in the saltwater. In fact, 90% of all creatures in the sea are bioluminescent.

FOXFIRE

Go for a walk in the woods during a dark, moonless night. Once your eyes adjust to the dark (after about 20 or 30 minutes), look carefully at the leaf-covered ground or the rotting wood of an old stump. You might see the eerie, soft glow of *foxfire*. Like the glow of fireflies, foxfire is also the result of bioluminescence. In this case, it is the byproduct of rapidly growing fungi that are eating the leaves or the stump.

Earth's average population density is 16 people per square mile.

WILL-O'-THE-WISPS

If you happen to be strolling through a marsh or walking along sea cliffs at night, you might see a will-o'-the-wisp. Some say they are caused by methane gas. Others believe they are the result of bioluminescence. Wisps might appear as a glowing ball or as many tiny flickers. They are almost always blue. If you're lucky and happen to see one, the wisp might seem to mimic your movement. When you move, the light moves; when you stop—so does the light. No wonder they're also called *fairy lights*.

EARTH LIGHTS

That's the name given to certain unexplained lights on our planet. Here are a few places you might spot these

Bald eagle nests (called *aeries*) can weigh over 2 tons—more than a car.

mysterious globes.

• **Hessdalen Valley Light, Norway.** You never know when, but sometimes during dark winter nights, the Hessdalen Valley lights up with dancing orbs of yellowish light. They appear all around the valley—even inside homes—but mostly they hover under the mountain ridges.

• **Hornet Ghost Light, Missouri.** The Hornet Ghost has been observed for more than 100 years. This orange ball of light is about the size of a basketball and swings about in the night sky, sometimes for as long as 30 minutes.

• **Brown Mountain Lights, North Carolina.** A German engineer first recorded seeing them in 1771, but according to Cherokee legend, the lights of Brown Mountain have been seen darting in and out of trees as far back as the year 1200. Their appearances are rare but unmistakable—the lights are visible for a few seconds at a time, starting out as blue or yellow, then fading to a dull red before disappearing. The best time to see them is during the fall.

So what—or *who*—is responsible for all this mysterious glowing? Ghosts? As-yet-unexplained scientific phenomena? Perhaps the future will shed some light…

*   *   *

GET THE LEAD OUT

In military contracts, pencils are sometimes referred to as "portable, handheld communications inscribers."

Q: What are the three largest Native American tribes in the U.S. today?

THE BERMUDA TRIANGLE

Ships go in... but they don't come out.

MYSTERIOUS WATERS

In 1492 Christopher Columbus sailed across the Atlantic Ocean on his first voyage to the New World. Near the island of Bermuda, he had compass trouble and observed strange lights. He noted it in his ship's log. Over the following centuries, other sailors had the same experience. Weird sounds were heard, and men and their boats sometimes disappeared from this place.

They call it the Bermuda Triangle—an area of ocean stretching from Bermuda to Florida to Puerto Rico and back. Even today, some people are afraid to sail or fly there. Some even call it the Devil's Triangle.

U.S.S. CYCLOPS

Stories have been told about this strange place for hundreds of years, but the Bermuda Triangle didn't become a legend until 1918. That was when a ship called the U.S.S. *Cyclops* sailed into the area and vanished, never to be heard from again.

How could a ship with 309 people on board just disappear? No trace of the ship was ever found. Not a lifeboat. Not a scrap of wood. Nothing.

A: 1) Cherokee, 2) Navajo, 3) Chippewa.

BOMBERS AWAY?

In 1945 five Avenger torpedo bombers left the Naval
Air Station in Ft. Lauderdale, Florida, and flew over that
area on a military exercise. Two hours into their flight,
they sent this radio message: "Everything is wrong. The
ocean doesn't look as it should." All five planes in the
squadron reported that their compasses were spinning.
They couldn't tell north from south. They said the sky
was a strange yellow color. And then they were gone.

The Navy immediately sent another plane with a crew
of 13 men to help them. That plane was never heard
from again, either. All six planes simply disappeared.

Where did they go? The Navy searched for weeks,
looking for an oil slick or a piece from a plane...but
nothing has ever been found.

WHERE'D EVERYBODY GO?

More than 100 ships and planes have passed into the
Triangle, never to be seen again. Ships have been found
drifting there with all of the people gone. Sometimes an
animal—like a dog or a bird—will be left on board, but
never any people. Sometimes pilots flying over the area
will be having a normal radio conversation with ground
control and suddenly they're gone. It's as if they've
flown into a hole in the sky.

Records show that more than 1,000 people have
been lost in the Bermuda Triangle. One possible explanation: It's a highly-trafficked area, so more disappear-
ances *would* occur. But does that explain everything?

Wild alligators are found in only two places in the world: the southern U.S. and Yangtze, China.

SPACE TOILETS

Space: the final frontier. The astronauts' mission:
To boldly go where no man has gone before.
The only question: How do they GO?

WET SUIT

In the early days of the U.S. space program, there were no space toilets. In fact, on the first named American space flight, Alan Shepard was supposed to be shot straight up and come straight down. They figured it would take only 15 minutes, so they didn't even think about supplying a bathroom. Unfortunately, the launch was delayed and Shepard was stuck in his space suit, lying on his back inside the capsule for hours. Finally, when he could hold it no longer, he just peed in his space suit.

SPACE DIAPERS

After Shepard's soggy experience, NASA came up with a new solution: they made an extra-large diaper for the second U.S. astronaut, Gus Grissom. And for the next 25 missions, astronauts wore a big plastic bag fastened directly to their bottoms with double-sided sticky tape.

ZERO-GRAV LAV

Today, space vehicles are equipped with a toilet called the Waste Collection System (WCS). It looks like the

---

A rocket must reach the speed of 7 miles per *second* to escape Earth's gravity.

ones we have on Earth but it's a little different. Toilets in space can't use water. Why? Because of weightlessness. Any basin (or bowl) of water would break into tiny little droplets and float around the space shuttle. So how do they make sure what goes into the toilet doesn't come out? They use a vacuum toilet. It works pretty much like a vacuum cleaner: When an astronaut pees, the urine is sucked away in a hose. When an astronaut poops, the astronaut pulls a lever to have the waste whisked away.

UNIVERSAL QUESTIONS

Where does the pee go? When the holding tank is filled with urine, it's dumped into space. This can be a spectacular sight. According to Apollo astronaut Russell Schweickart, "There is nothing quite as beautiful as a urine dump at sunset." The instant the urine goes out the exit nozzle, it freezes into millions of little ice crystals. And because space is essentially a perfect vacuum, those crystals blast off in every direction at a really high speed. "It's an incredible stream," says Russell. "A spray of sparklers."

Where does the poop go? All solid waste is freeze-dried and deodorized. Then it is kept in plastic bags and taken back to Earth to be analyzed. Why do they analyze it? Scientists want to know what effect space travel has on bodily functions.

Reflect on this: A chimpanzee can learn to recognize himself in a mirror—monkeys can't.

A-M-A-Z-I-N-G A-N-A-G-R-A-M-S

An anagram is a word or phrase made by rearranging the letters of another word or phrase. Check out these.

Television set *becomes* See? It's not live.

A volcanic eruption *becomes* Topic: cone, lava, ruin.

Charlie's Angels *becomes* Lean girls chase.

Be all that you can be *becomes* Obey, launch a battle.

Yosemite Valley *becomes* Yes, a lovely time!

Schoolmaster *becomes* The classroom.

Butterfly *becomes* Flutter by.

The Addams Family *becomes* My dismal fathead.

Gosh, see that triangle? *becomes* It has got three angles.

Computer science *becomes* Concrete scum pie.

Made in America *becomes* I am a nice dream.

Shel Silverstein *becomes* I sell thin verses.

A Nintendo Game Boy *becomes* Made to be annoying.

Original name for Hostess Twinkies: Little Shortcake Fingers.

REEL SILLY

More wit than wisdom from the movies.

"I'm a Mog: Half man, half dog. I'm my own best friend!"
—**Barf, Spaceballs**

"We're babies! We're supposed to get in trouble. That's our job!"
—**Tommy, Rugrats**

"Okay. I don't need a compass to tell me which way the wind shines."
—**Furious, Mystery Men**

"And then one time I ate some rotten berries. Man there were some gases eeking outta my butt that day!"
—**Donkey, Shrek**

"Don't torture yourself, Gomez. That's my job."
—**Morticia, The Addams Family**

"Invention, my dear friends, is 93% perspiration, 6% electricity, 4% evaporation, and 2% Butterscotch Ripple."
—**Willy Wonka, Willy Wonka and the Chocolate Factory**

"Waiter, I'm in my soup!"
—**Fly, A Bug's Life**

"Whoever said orange was the new pink was seriously disturbed."
—**Elle Woods, Legally Blonde**

"Well the buzz from the bees is that the leopards are in a bit of a spot. The baboons are going ape. I told the elephants to forget it, but they can't."
—**Zazu, The Lion King**

Q: How many bananas does it take to make a pint of "banana oil?"

PHOBIAS

Do you know someone who is so afraid of spiders that they
scream whenever they see one, no matter how small it is?
Or do you know someone who is afraid to fly in a plane?
Overwhelming fears like these are called phobias.

E VERYONE'S AFRAID OF SOMETHING

No one really knows why people suffer from phobias, but brain chemistry and heredity might have something to do with it.

Some phobias have been around forever, like *nyctophobia*, the fear of the dark, or *brontophobia*, fear of thunder and lightning. Some fears are more commonly known, like *claustrophobia*, fear of small enclosed spaces, or *acrophobia*, the fear of heights. Other phobias are so new they don't even have names yet—like the fear of garbage disposals or the fear of driving on the highway. Some people even suffer from the fear of taking those little cotton balls out of new medicine bottles.

TEST YOUR PHOBIA I.Q.

Just for fun, Uncle John has put together a phobia quiz. Your task is to match the fear with the phobia. Some phobias you might recognize

A: None—"banana oil" is made from petroleum.

right away. Others might be more difficult. But have no fear—the answers are provided.

And, if you are afraid that some of the names of phobias are just too long to even guess at, take a look at this phobia: the fear of long words is called *hippopotomonstrosesquippedaliophobia*. (Try saying that 10 times fast!)

MATCH THE FEAR WITH THE PHOBIA

Fear	Phobia
1. Fear of spiders	a. Necrophobia
2. Fear of telephones	b. Cyberphobia
3. Fear of insects	c. Motorphobia
4. Fear of flying	d. Hydrophobia
5. Fear of computers	e. Phonophobia
6. Fear of animals	f. Dentophobia
7. Fear of automobiles	g. Aviophobia
8. Fear of water	h. Entomophobia
9. Fear of dentists	i. Arachnophobia
10. Fear of death	j. Zoophobia

Answers

1. i; 2. e; 3. h; 4. g; 5. b; 6. j; 7. c; 8. d; 9. f; 10. a.

*   *   *

"The only thing we have to fear is fear itself."

—**Franklin D. Roosevelt**

Snakes can have as many as 450 vertebrae, each with a pair of ribs.

TOYS 'R' WEIRD

*Behind every toy is a story. And sometimes the story
is as interesting as the toy itself—especially when
the story involves grown-ups acting stupid.*

BOBBLEHEADS

Believe it or not, bobbleheads have been around for more than 400 years. Papier maché bobbleheads were made in China in the 1600s and they've gone in and out of style ever since.

The most recent bobblehead craze began in 1999, when the San Francisco Giants gave away Willie Mays bobblehead dolls. Then the Minnesota Twins gave out four different bobbleheads. Other teams followed. When the Philadelphia 76ers offered Allen Iverson bobbleheads to the first 5,000 kids at a game, it was total chaos. Bobblehead collectors were actually renting children so they could get one of the dolls!

Today, more than a million bobbleheads are made every month. Where are they made? In China...the country where bobbleheads first began.

CABBAGE PATCH KIDS

In 1978 a 23-year-old artist named Xavier Roberts started creating soft-sculpture dolls by hand. The dolls had pudgy faces, stumpy arms, and small, close-set eyes.

They were completely different from the traditional cute baby doll. He called them Little People Originals. But he didn't "sell" them—he let people pay a fee to "adopt" them. He and five friends bought an old medical clinic in Georgia, renamed it Babyland General Hospital, and opened it to the public.

Assistants dressed as nurses helped customers adopt their very own "baby" by giving them birth certificates with the doll's name and "birth date." They even passed out official-looking adoption papers. Little People were an immediate hit.

Doll Crazy

Four years later, Roberts signed a deal with a major toy manufacturer, Coleco Toys, and changed the name of the dolls to Cabbage Patch Kids. With a vinyl head and a slightly smaller size than the Little People, each was unique—during the manufacturing process, a computer randomly placed small changes in each doll. Kids loved it!

The dolls were such a hot Christmas item in 1983 that supplies ran low. Fistfights broke out between customers desperate to get a doll. Because there weren't enough dolls to go around, many stores held lotteries to decide who could buy one. Police had to be called in to keep shoppers from rioting.

More than $600 million worth of Cabbage Patch Kids sold in 1985, making them the most successful toy of the 1980s.

YIN AND YANG

*This ancient symbol represents the opposing forces of
the universe, known as yin and yang. The ancient religon
called Taoism (pronounced dow-ism) teaches that harmony
in the universe comes from balancing opposites such as
good and evil, warm and cold, male and female, and
darkness and light. This story, from the Chinese,
tells how that balance happened.*

THE EGG

In the beginning of time, there was only chaos, fighting and churning inside an enormous egg. One day the egg broke and a giant called Pan Ku appeared. With him came the two basic forces: Yin and Yang.

Yin, the dark energy, sank down and became the Earth. Yang, the light energy, floated up and became Heaven. Yin and Yang, being complete opposites, wanted to fight with each other.

But Pan Ku would not let them—he stood between them and pushed them apart.

Every year Pan Ku grew taller and stronger, and Heaven and Earth were pushed farther and farther apart. At last, after 18,000 years, Pan Ku had grown so large and Heaven and Earth were so far apart that they could no longer hurt each other.

THE EARTH

When Pan Ku's work was

finally finished, he was very, very old and very tired. So the giant lay down upon the Earth and prepared to die. As he died, a miracle happened: Pan Ku's hands and feet became the four quarters of the globe. His head turned into the mountains that rise up from the Earth. His right eye became the sun and his left eye, the moon.

A thousand different plants and trees grew from his skin and hair. Pan Ku's blood made the rivers and the sea. His teeth, bones, and marrow became the metals, rocks, and precious stones within the Earth. From his breath came the winds and from his booming voice came thunder.

Last of all came the people. They were created from the fleas and lice that crept all over Pan Ku's hairy body.

And that is how the world began.

Picasso created about 13,500 works of art in his 78-year career. (That's one every other day.)

WHERE IT'S @

E-mail has only been around for a few decades; but @ (the "at" sign) has been around for centuries.

A BRIEF HISTORY OF @

Some linguists say the @ sign first appeared in the Middle Ages, when monks used it to shorten the Latin word *ad*, which means "at, toward, or by." Others claim that @ stood for a measurement of weight in Spain in the 1400s. The measurement was "a jar" of something, or an *arroba*. Yet another view says @ was used by market sellers in the 1700s to show how much something might cost. They put signs in front of their stands, like "5 POTATOES @ 10 PENCE." Two hundred years later, that symbol of the marketplace made its way to the keyboard of the first Underwood typewriter. It was called the *commercial "a."*

INTO THE DIGITAL AGE

When computer programmer Ray Tomlinson invented electronic mail in 1972, he had to come up with a system for addresses. He needed to find a character to separate the name of the user from the network domain. It could not be a symbol that might be used in spelling someone's name.

Tomlinson studied the keyboard and found @. It was perfect: people would never spell their names with it, and it signified "at." So his e-mail address could be, for

---

Thirsty? Head north—about 25% of the world's fresh water is in Canada's lakes and rivers.

example, Ray@home. In 1971 Ray sent his first electronic message—to himself.

Nowadays, the only problem with @ is what to call it. In Spain, it's still called *arroba*, a holdover from the jar measurement. The French use a modified version of that word: *arobase*. North Americans and the British call it the *at sign*. Translated into German, that's *at-Zichen*. In Japanese, it's *atto maak*.

Other people are more creative. They've come up with names describing what it looks like:

French	*petit escargot*	"little snail"
Swedish	*kanelbulle*	"cinnamon bun"
Danish	*snabel-a*	"the 'a' with the elephant's trunk"
Finnish	*miukumauku*	"sign of the meow" (for a curled-up sleeping cat)

* * *

MORE TXT TLK (for instant messaging)

6	Parent over shoulder	ATM	At the moment
66	They're gone	GR8	Great
BAK	Back at keyboard	B4	Before
WB	Welcome back	UW	You wish
EG	Evil grin	BBS	Be back soon
UKW	You know who	GFY	Good for you
D	The	B4N	Bye for now

FAMILY HOLIDAYS

Every year, North Americans set aside special days to honor our fathers, our mothers, and even our grand-parents. How did these holidays get started?

MOTHER'S DAY (second Sunday in May)
Origin: In 1908 Anna Jarvis, a West Virginia schoolteacher, started a one-woman crusade in honor of her mother, who had died three years earlier. On May 10, 1908, Jarvis persuaded pastors in several nearby cities to hold Mother's Day services in their churches. From there she launched a letter-writing campaign to governors, congressmen, clergy, and the media. Six years later she finally achieved her goal: on May 9, 1914, President Woodrow Wilson issued an official proclamation establishing the holiday.

The Inside Scoop: Jarvis—who had no children of her own—came to hate the holiday she created. She loathed its commercialism, especially flowers and greeting cards. "Any mother would rather have a line of the worst scribble from her son or daughter," she complained, "than a fancy greeting card."

FATHER'S DAY (third Sunday in June)

Origin: Anna Jarvis's idea inspired a Spokane, Washington, housewife named Sonora Dodd to work for a

Father's Day in honor of her dad, who had raised six children alone. She proposed making Father's Day the first Sunday in June—the month of her father's birthday. But local religious leaders needed more time to prepare appropriate sermons, so they settled on the third Sunday. The first Father's Day: June 19, 1910.

Although President Wilson personally observed the holiday, he refused to make it official. And no succeeding president would officially endorse the holiday, either. The reason: They feared voters would think it was too self-serving. Finally in 1972, Father's Day was proclaimed a federal holiday by President Richard Nixon.

The Inside Scoop: Although she turned down many offers to endorse products, Dodd had nothing against giving gifts on Father's Day. "After all," she said, "why should the greatest giver of gifts not be on the receiving end at least once a year?"

GRANDPARENTS' DAY (first Sunday after Labor Day)

Origin: Most historians give credit for this holiday to Marian McQuade, a grandmother from West Virginia. But others say it was Michael Goldgar, a grandfather from Georgia. Both made several trips to Washington to lobby for a holiday that celebrated the wisdom of grandparents. Whichever it was, it worked. President Carter signed Grandparent's Day into law in 1978. September was chosen because it represents the autumn years of life.

Every year, Americans spend $20 million on Father's Day ties.

DEAD OR ALIVE?

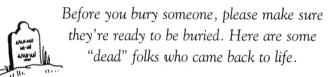

*Before you bury someone, please make sure
they're ready to be buried. Here are some
"dead" folks who came back to life.*

Pronounced Dead: Margaret Erskine of Scotland
What Happened: Erskine was pronounced dead
in 1574. She was given a somber funeral and was
then buried in the family tomb. That night, the cemetery caretaker snuck into the tomb and tried to steal the
ring off Margaret's finger. He was given the fright of his
life when the dead woman sat up in her coffin and let
loose a blood-curdling scream. Erskine recovered and
lived for another 51 years. The caretaker, on the other
hand, was probably never the same again.

Pronounced Dead: Matthew Wall of England
What Happened: Wall was a farmer in the 16th century. When he died, he was put into a wooden coffin and
carried to the cemetery. But the clumsy pallbearers
slipped on some wet leaves and accidentally dropped
the coffin on the road (Fleece Lane), somehow knocking the life back into Wall. Years later, when he finally
did pass away, the farmer provided in his will for Fleece
Lane to be swept clean every year on the anniversary of
his revival—October 2. The townspeople still celebrate
Old Man's Day to commemorate that lucky
old farmer, Matthew Wall.

It's a dirty job, but someone's got to do it: A *garbologist* is a scientist who studies garbage.

Pronounced Dead: James Bartley, a 36-year-old sailor

What Happened: In 1891 Bartley, a crewman of the British whaling ship *Star of the East*, was swallowed by a sperm whale. His mates quickly harpooned the whale, badly injuring it, but were unable to save poor Bartley. The next day, the whale was found dead, floating on the surface of the water. The crew hauled it aboard, sliced it open, and were shocked to find seaman Bartley—unconscious, but still breathing—in the whale's stomach!

Bartley was delirious for days but recovered to describe his ordeal. He remembered being in darkness, then slipping along a passage to a larger space, and then being covered in slime. Not only that, his tan skin had been bleached white by the whale's gastric juices.

Pronounced Dead: Glenda Stevens's dog, Sweetie

What Happened: Glenda was heartbroken when a mail truck hit her little dog. She checked carefully for a heartbeat, but when she didn't hear one, she tearfully buried her beloved pet in the backyard. Hours later, Glenda's daughter looked outside and saw Sweetie's legs sticking out of the ground. Sweetie, who wasn't dead after all, was actually digging herself out of the grave!

First European to explore North America: a Viking named Leif Eriksson, in about 1000 A.D.

C-O-D-E BREAKERS

Can you figure out this message from Uncle John?

R VLLF WLST! BLLG BL CG GWKLL E'ISEIQ

VLCK GWL GWKEVL KEEB.

TSLCUL HL GWLKL CVF FEV'G HL SCGL.

C ULIKLG UYKTKRUL MRSS ZKLLG AEY.

HKRVZ GWL TSYVZLK!

HOW TO BE A CODE BREAKER

1. Count the types of characters. If it has 12 to 50 different ones, it's probably based on an alphabet (this message is based on the English alphabet).

2. Which letter occurs most often? (In English, it's E.)

3. Put E wherever the most frequent character comes.

4. Now guess which three signs create the word *the*—the most common three-letter word in English.

5. When you're sure of #4, put T and H in their proper places. This should suggest some other words (*there, their, these, then*, etc.)

By now you probably have enough letters to solve the coded message.

Answer on page 283.

Run, Kermit! Giant water bugs, which grow to 4 inches long, can eat frogs.

SPORTS GREATS

Want to be a sports superstar? It's easy! Well, actually, no, it's not. It takes hard work and determination. And it doesn't hurt to have extraordinary physical skills, too.

WHAT MAKES BARRY BONDS GREAT?

Barry Bonds of the San Francisco Giants is the best hitter in baseball. He's hit more home runs in a season than any other baseball player and he won the 2002 National League Batting Crown. He's not the biggest; he's not the strongest; he's not even the fastest. So what's his secret? Excellent eyesight.

Most people have 20/20 vision. Barry has 20/13 vision. That means he has better than average vision—he can see at 20 feet what someone else can see at 13. Barry says he can see the stitches on the baseball the second it leaves the pitcher's hand. He can see how the ball spins in the air, which lets him know if the pitch is a fastball, a slider, or a curveball. Once Barry knows what kind of ball is coming toward him, he decides whether to swing at it. And Barry has the batting power to knock those balls out of the park.

WHAT MADE WILMA RUDOLF GREAT?

Wilma Rudolf was known as the fastest woman in history. In the 1960 Olympics, she won three gold medals in track. Only eight years before—when she was 12—Wilma had been unable to walk without a leg brace because of polio, a disease that paralyzed her left leg. Doctors told her she would never walk again, but Wilma refused to listen to them. She worked hard and not only learned to walk again, she learned to run. Then she started to compete. At first, Wilma lost every race, but she never gave up. She became a star on her high school basketball team, then became a star on her college track team. She worked hard and by the time she was 16, the Tennessee Tornado (as she was called) was asked to join the U.S. Olympic track team. Four years later she made Olympic history. What made Wilma great? Determination, hard work, and a fierce belief in herself.

WHAT MADE MICHAEL JORDAN GREAT?

Michael Jordan is one of the most recognized athletes in the world. He led his team, the Chicago Bulls, to the NBA championship six times! His amazing prowess on the basketball court earned him the nicknames "Air Jordan," and "his Airness." But winning isn't as easy as it sometimes looks. As Jordan himself said, "I have missed more than 9,000 shots in my career. I have lost almost 300 games. Twenty-six times, I've been trusted to take the game-winning shot… and missed. I've failed over and over and over again in my life. And that is why I succeed."

WHAT MADE PELE GREAT?

Brazilian-born Pelé (pronounced Pay-lay) is one of the greatest soccer players who ever lived. He was most known for his "bicycle kick," in which he kicked the ball backward over his head and into the goal. Doctors were so amazed by his physical abilities that they performed tests on him to find out what made him such a great player. They discovered that besides having perfect motor skills and great speed, Pele also had unusually keen peripheral vision, which is the vision that allows you to see out the sides of your eyes. This meant he was able to see most of the soccer field while he was playing. (Talk about keeping your eye on the ball!) Doctors also discovered that Pele had a genius I.Q. He loved to play chess and worked on geometry problems whenever he could. That kind of problem-solving skill—along with his great vision and speed—really helped Pelé master his game.

WHAT MAKES LANCE ARMSTRONG GREAT?

Lance says he was born to race bikes. He was 13 when he won the Kids Iron Triathlon. By the time he was 22 he was known as the "Golden Boy of American Cycling." Then, in 1996, he received the devastating news that he had cancer…and would probably die.

Lance refused to accept that. And amazingly, three operations and several rounds of chemotherapy later, he was back on his bicycle. Still, many top bike teams were afraid to let him join. They thought he'd be weak and unable to compete. Again, Lance refused to accept it. His absolute belief in himself made him the winner he is today. Not only has he won his battle with cancer, he's won the Tour de France—the most famous and difficult bike race in the world—four times!

Hole in one! LifeSavers are the most popular non-chocolate candy in the U.S.

IF THE SHOE FITS

Q: What have tongues but never speak? A: Shoes, of course. You put them on every day, but have you ever wondered about their origin? Here are a few fascinating shoe facts.

FASHION POLICE

• In the 1300s, Philip the Fair, king of France, passed a law that forbade anyone in his court—counts, dukes, barons, and their wives—to own more than four outfits. Philip forgot to mention shoes in his law, so these nobles spent enormous amounts of money on shoes.

In fact, shoe fashions became so wild that at one point they had two-foot-long tips. These really long tips were reserved for princes and nobility. The merely rich were allowed only one-foot-long tips, and lower-class folks could have six-inch toes. This fashion ended abruptly in 1396 during the Battle of Nicopolis, when people had to cut the tips off their shoes to run away.

• **Quack!** And speaking of French shoes, in the 1400s, men's shoes had a square tip that looked like a duck's bill. This fashion was started by King Charles VIII to hide the fact that he had six toes on one foot.

• **That's hot!** Heeled shoes made their first appearance in the Middle East, not as a fashion statement, but to lift the foot off the burning sand. Ancient Romans wore "platform shoes" to keep their feet out of water and mud.

Get started! Composer Johann Sebastian Bach started playing the violin at age 4.

- **Cave fashions.** How long have people been wearing boots? A cave painting dating from 13,000 B.C. was found in Spain, depicting a man and a woman wearing knee-high boots of fur and animal skin.

- **High anxiety.** During the 1500s and 1600s in Europe, the heels on shoes were always colored red. Upper-class women wore heels as high as six inches—which lifted them so high up and so off-balance that they needed servants to help them walk.

- **Sealing the deal.** In Biblical times, a sandal was given as a gift to symbolize an agreed-upon promise. In the Middle Ages, when a man asked a woman to marry him, the bride-to-be's father would give the suitor one of his daughter's shoes. During the wedding, the groom would give his bride the shoe, which she would put on to show her that husband now ruled her. (Remind you of Cinderella?) Today shoes are sometimes tied to the bumpers of newlyweds' cars—a holdover from that shoe ceremony from nearly 1,000 years ago.

- **Right on?** Back in 200 A.D., the Romans were the first to make shoes for right and left feet. But that concept got lost and shoes were one-size-fits-both-feet for the next 1,600 years. Then, in 1839, William Young, a shoemaker in Philadelphia, Pennsylvania, decided there was a difference between feet after all and designed shoes for each foot. He became known as the "crooked shoemaker."

Times change: In 1915 schoolteachers weren't allowed to date, smoke, or go out after dark.

ANIMAL ACTS

*They say the best offense is a good defense...
especially when the defense is really offensive!*

BARFING BIRDS. Petrels are pigeon-size natives of Antarctica that defend their nests by throwing up on predators. They have two stomachs: one for digesting food—mostly fish or shrimp—and another for storing a special orange oil. They can barf that orange goo a distance of three feet and sometimes farther. If you happen to be the target of the petrel's vomit, good luck washing it off. You'll stink like fish...for days.

PEEING FROGS. Some kinds of frogs release a foul-smelling (and foul-tasting) pee that they hope will keep any hungry animals from eating them.

FARTING SNAKES. Some snakes hiss or rattle to warn enemies away. But have you ever heard of a snake that farts? The Sonoran coral snake and the western hook-nosed snake both fart when they feel threatened. Scientists use the polite term *cloacal popping*, but it's the same thing as farting. Snake "pops" sound very much like human farts, except that they are slightly higher in pitch. Does it work? Predators usually have the same reaction to farts as the rest of us: they run!

Q: What's one thing that snakes can do, but insects can't?   A: Sneeze.

WISE GUYS

We gave you "Reel Wisdom" on page 14. Now ponder some real wisdom from history's best-known philosophers.

"You can discover more about a person in an hour of play than in a year of conversation."
—**Plato (427–347 B.C.)**

"Our greatest glory is not in never falling, but in rising every time we fall."
—**Confucius (551–479 B.C.)**

"Teaching should be such that what is offered is perceived as a valuable gift and not as a hard duty."
—**Albert Einstein (1879–1955)**

"He who fights against monsters should see to it that he does not become a monster in the process."
—**Friedrich Nietzsche (1844–1900)**

"Do not do to others what angers you if done to *you* by others."
—**Socrates (469–399 B.C.)**

"He is able who thinks he is able."
—**Buddha (566–486 B.C.)**

"A friend might well be reckoned the masterpiece of nature."
—**Ralph Waldo Emerson (1803–1882)**

"We are what we repeatedly do. Excellence, then, is not an act, but a habit."
—**Aristotle (384–322 B.C.)**

"It is not enough to have a good mind. The main thing is to use it well."
—**René Descartes (1596–1650)**

Lucky break: Marilyn Monroe got her start when she was crowned Artichoke Queen in 1947.

VIDEO TREASURES

Ever found yourself at a video store with no idea what to get? Here are a few recommendations.

THE BLACK STALLION (1979) *Drama*
"A young boy and a wild Arabian stallion are the only survivors of a shipwreck, and they develop a deep affection for each other. Great for adults and kids." (*VideoHound's Golden Movie Retriever*)

INTO THE WEST (1993) *Fantasy*
"An odd, likeable film about a father who hunts for his two sons who have run away from their Dublin, Ireland, home with a mythical white horse, Tir na nOg." (*Halliwell's Film and Video Guide*)

IRRECONCILABLE DIFFERENCES (1984) *Drama*
"When her Beverly Hills parents spend more time working and fretting than giving hugs and love, a 10-year-old girl (Drew Barrymore) sues them for divorce." (*VideoHound's Golden Movie Retriever*)

THE MUPPET MOVIE (1979) *Comedy*
"Kermit the Frog, Fozzie Bear, and the rest of the loveably fuzzy characters created by Jim Henson embark on a wacky quest for stardom in this appealing children's adventure." (*All Movie Guide*)

It's against the law to slurp your soup in public in New Jersey. (At home it's okay.)

WILLOW (1988) *Fantasy*

"Rollicking fantasy-adventure about a little person who takes on the challenge of shepherding an abandoned baby to its place of destiny—where it will destroy the evil powers of Queen Bavmorda." (*Leonard Maltin's Movie & Video Guide*)

THE IRON GIANT (1999) *Animated Adventure*

"The setting is 1957; a large fireball plunges from space into the ocean off the coast of Maine. The visitor turns out to be a massive robot, designed as a 'living weapon'— but disoriented enough to befriend a nine-year-old boy in this enchanting tale." (*Video Movie Guide*)

WARGAMES (1983) *Suspense*

"Sooner or later, some computer is going to blow us all off the face of the planet. That's the theme of this intelligent thriller. A computer whiz (Matthew Broderick) accidentally hacks into the government's mainframe and challenges it to play 'Global Thermonuclear Warfare.' It cheerfully agrees." (*Roger Ebert's Home Movie Companion*)

EVER AFTER (1998) *Fantasy*

"A charming rethinking of the classic fairy tale *Cinderella*, with Drew Barrymore as a feisty orphan who puts her potential Prince Charming to shame with her bravery and regard for humankind." (*Leonard Maltin's Movie & Video Guide*)

ELEPHANTS, PART 2

On page 81 we told you how elephants are a lot like humans. So what do elephants have that makes them so special? Two things: big brains and amazing trunks.

THEY NEVER FORGET

An elephant brain—like the human brain—is large and complex. Almost all other mammals have smaller brains compared to the size of their body, so they must rely more on *instincts*, or built-in instructions, to guide them. But elephants' oversized brains allow them to learn and to pass on knowledge. This also gives them great memories—elephants can recognize other elephants, people, places, and objects that they haven't seen for years.

NO BONES ABOUT IT

But it's the elephant's trunk that makes it so unique. And what exactly is a trunk? A lip? Not entirely. A nose? Kind of.

The trunk is actually a union of a nose *and* an upper lip—a highly sensitive, multitalented appendage that contains more than 100,000 muscles and not a single bone.

On the tip of the trunk are two fleshy buds that act like fingers. They allow an elephant to pick up a single peanut from the ground or remove tiny bugs from their

A human skull is actually made up of 8 bones that fit together like a jigsaw puzzle.

skin. But the trunk is also very powerful. An adult elephant's trunk can be seven feet long and weigh more than *300 pounds*—and be strong enough to knock down an entire tree!

The trunk is also an incredible sensory organ, giving elephants a better sense of smell than any other land mammal. And with the huge brain to guide it, the trunk can be put to hundreds of different uses. Here are a few:

Disciplinary Tool: Mother gently trunk-slaps her child.

Toy: Why did Junior get slapped? Because he was using his trunk to fling mud on Mom.

Bucket: A trunk can suck in more than a gallon of water to drink or wash with.

Snorkel: Elephants can walk along the bottom of a river with just the tip of their trunks sticking out for air.

Crane: If an elephant needs to reach higher, she'll use her trunk to stack a pile of logs or rocks to stand on.

Paintbrush: Elephants in captivity have been taught to paint pictures with their trunks. Some have been shown in museums and sold for thousands of dollars!

So the next time you see an elephant in a zoo or at a game park, say hello. Chances are, your greeting will be appreciated.

Are you left-handed? If so, there's about a 50% chance that you're left-footed, too.

SUPERSTITIOUS?

This handy guide may get you through the day.

GETTING OUT OF BED. When you woke up, did you get out of bed on the same side you got in the night before? It's bad luck if you didn't.

AT THE BREAKFAST TABLE. Did you spill some salt at breakfast? It is said that for every grain scattered, a tear will fall. Toss a pinch of the spilled salt over your left shoulder; otherwise, bad luck will follow.

ON YOUR WAY TO SCHOOL. Was a black cat walking toward you this morning? If so, it was bringing good luck. If it was walking the other way…well, too bad for you. All your good luck just walked away.

IN SCHOOL. When you took that math test, did you use the same pencil that you used to study with? If so, you're in luck—the pencil remembered the answers.

ON YOUR WAY HOME FROM SCHOOL. Did you see an ambulance? That's very unlucky…unless you remembered to pinch your nose or hold your breath until you saw a brown or black dog.

DOING CHORES. Did you sweep the dirt out the door…after dark? If you did, a stranger is bound to visit.

GOING TO BED. Did you trip up the stairs on your way to bed? Guess what? You're going to fall in love soon!

Start your engines: The average house cat spends 10,950 hours purring in its lifetime.

THOMAS EDISON

The next time you switch on an electric light or go to the movies, think of Thomas Edison. Because without him, you'd be sitting in the dark, watching nothing.

UNDERACHIEVER

Thomas Alva Edison, or Al, as his friends called him, was one of the greatest inventors of all time. He was born in Ohio in 1847 but moved to Port Huron, Michigan, when he was just a boy. Those who knew him in those early days were later surprised to hear that he had made something of himself. Why? He was considered an odd child. He was extremely curious and always getting himself into trouble.

He had scarlet fever when he was a baby which damaged his hearing and may have caused learning disabilities. His first teacher said that his brain was addled and he really shouldn't be in school. Even Edison's father thought he was stupid. But his mother, Nancy Edison, believed in him, so she home-schooled Al—which was the best thing that ever happened to him.

MOTHER KNOWS BEST

When Al was nine, his mother brought home a book, R. G. Parker's *School of Natural and Experimental Philosophy*, which had lots of scientific experiments that could be done at home. That was it! He did every single experiment. Then he begged for more books and spent every penny he could earn on chemicals. From then on, Al's mom bought him books…but Al taught himself.

BOY GENIUS

At 12, Al worked selling sandwiches, fruit, and candy to passengers on the Grand Trunk Railroad. He got on the train in the morning, spent the day in Detroit, and returned later that same night. It was a long time to be away from home, so the conductor let him set up a lab in the baggage car, where he could carry out experiments while he waited for the return trip.

When his chemicals caught fire one day, it put an end to the baggage-car lab, but that didn't stop Al. He set up a printing press (also in the baggage car) and printed his own newspaper on the train. He called it *The Grand Trunk Weekly Herald*. The year was 1862 and people were anxious to read stories about the Civil War.

One morning, Al saved a little boy from being killed by a runaway boxcar. The boy's father was the stationmaster and was so grateful that he offered to teach Al how to use the telegraph machine. In typical fashion, Al learned to be a first-rate telegrapher, built his own equipment, and became Port Huron's official telegraph operator. And with his knowledge of the telegraph, he had all the tools he needed to start changing the world.

MOVIN' ON UP

When Al Edison hit 21, he moved to New York to become an inventor. While working for Western

Union, he made improved versions of the telegraph and the typewriter. Then he invented an electric pen that made copies of documents. In 1869 he sold several of his inventions, including the "stock ticker"—a machine that gave up-to-the-minute information about stocks and the price of gold and silver—to the Gold and Stock Company for the whopping sum of $40,000. With that money, Edison created the world's first industrial research laboratory in Menlo Park, New Jersey.

THE WIZARD OF MENLO PARK

Edison's lab had workshops, a machine shop, a chemistry lab, a library full of technical books, and storerooms. It even had a glassblower's house and a rooming house where many of his workers lived.

Though he was married and had children, Edison's life revolved around the lab. In fact, there were many nights when he slept on top of a lab table. And when Edison wasn't at work, he carried a yellow notebook and would stop in the middle of dinner or a conversation and scribble down an idea or a drawing for an invention. In his lifetime he filled more than 3,000 notepads. "I find out what the world needs," he said. "Then I go ahead and try and invent it."

ANYTHING YOU CAN DO...

Edison's work led to invention after invention, and he became known as the "Wizard of Menlo Park." When Alexander Graham Bell invented the telephone, Edison improved it. He invented a microphone and transmitter that made a voice come through loud and clear. In 1877 he invented a machine that could record sounds and then replay them: the phonograph.

LIGHTING UP THE WORLD

In 1878 Edison began looking for a way to use electricity to light homes. He filled hundreds of notebooks with his ideas. "I speak without exaggeration," he said, "when I say that I have considered 3,000 theories in connection with electric light."

Other inventors had tried to pass electric current through glass bulbs, but none of them worked very well. Edison was determined to succeed where they had failed. He experimented for more than a year trying to get a lightbulb that would glow brightly and not burn out.

Finally, in 1879, Edison perfected the electric lightbulb. It was his greatest invention. He strung lights from his workshop to the trees and houses all around Menlo Park, and soon the whole town was glowing.

In 1882 he installed a power plant in New York City and suddenly people were able to turn night into day with the flick of a switch. The success of that plant led Edison to build power plants in other cities. His invention electrified the nation and soon, the world.

HE KEPT GOING...AND GOING...AND...

Did Thomas Edison stop with that magnificent invention? Of course not. He also invented the movie camera, the movie projector, a talking doll, the car battery, electric meters, motors, pumps, generators, an electric railroad, and robot torpedoes, to mention just a few. In all, he is credited with more than 1,000 inventions.

He continued to create and invent until his dying day, saying, "I am long on ideas but short on time." When the Wizard of Menlo Park passed away at 84, President Hoover honored him by having all the houses and offices across the country dim their lights as a farewell to this very bright star.

*　　*　　*

FIRST WORDS...

• **On the telegraph:** Samuel B. Morse, the inventor of the telegraph, sent the first telegraph message on May 24, 1844. His message: "What hath God wrought?"

• **On the telephone:** The world's first phone call was on March 10, 1876, when Alexander Graham Bell telephoned his assistant, Mr. Watson. What did he say? "Mr. Watson, come here; I want you."

• **By e-mail:** Sometime in 1972, Ray Tomlinson sent the very first e-mail message—to himself. What was the text of this historic message? Tomlinson doesn't really remember, but thinks it was the top row of letters on the keyboard, "qwertyuiop."

ANIMA-LISTS

*Here's one of our pet projects—some
ideas for naming your pet.*

MOST POPULAR DOG NAMES	FAMOUS FICTIONAL DOGS	MOST POPULAR CAT NAMES
Girl dog	Snoopy	**Boy cat**
Lady	Lassie	Max
Maggie	Benji	Sam
Sadie	Rin Tin Tin	Simba
Molly	Scooby Doo	Charlie
Brandy	Old Yeller	Oliver
Princess	Clifford	Oscar
Samantha	Lady	Gizmo
Sheba	Beethoven	Buddy
Sandy	Hooch	Toby
Missy		Spike
	DOG or CAT PAIRS	
Boy dog		**Girl cat**
Max	Ben & Jerry	Sassy
Buddy	Beauty & Beast	Misty
Bear	Cookies & Cream	Princess
Shadow		Samantha
Bailey	Frank & Stein	Lucy
Jake	Peeka & Boo	Missy
Rocky	Barbie & Ken	Molly
Duke	Rock & Roll	Sophie
Lucky	Peanut Butter & Jelly	Pumpkin
Rusty		Maggie

Camels are native to North America.

SPORTS SUPERSTITIONS

Why did Babe Ruth touch second base every time he came in from right field? For good luck. Why did Willie Mays avoid it? Bad luck. Apparently some athletes don't trust their skills alone. Here are some other strange sports superstitions.

BASEBALL

- It's good luck to spit in your hand before you pick up the bat.
- Never lend your bat to another player.
- If a dog walks across the diamond before the first pitch, that's very bad luck.

BASKETBALL

- The last person to shoot a basket during the warm-up will have a good game.
- Bounce the ball before a foul shot. That's good luck.

RODEO

- Always put your right foot in the stirrup first.
- Never kick a paper cup thrown down on the rodeo ground.
- If you put your hat on a bed—you'll be seriously injured that day.
- Don't wear yellow.

TENNIS

- It's bad luck to hold more than two balls at a time when you're serving.
- When you switch sides, walk around the outside of the court.
- Don't wear yellow.

Purrrfect double: Scientists cloned a cat in 2001. It's name is cc—short for carbon copy.

GOLF

• Use only odd-numbered clubs when you start your game.

• Carry some coins in your pocket. That's good luck.

• Golf balls have numbers on them so you can tell which is yours. It's bad luck to use one that has a number higher than four.

FISHING

• Throw back your first catch for good luck.

• Don't change rods while fishing—it's bad luck.

• If you spit on your bait before you cast your rod, the fish will bite.

• If a barefoot woman passes you on your way to the dock, go home—the fish won't bite.

* * *

SPORTS SHORTS

• Did you know there were hooligans (troublemakers like the father and son who jumped out of the stands and attacked the first base coach at a baseball game in 2002) at sports games 2,000 years ago? Roman writer Tacitus reported battles between rival team supporters in Pompeii's amphitheater in the first century A.D.

• Naked fact: Olympians always wore clothing until a runner's loincloth fell off during a race in 720 B.C. He kept going, and won the race. Like athletes of any era, the losers copied the techniques of the winner, so subsequent competitions were held without clothes.

SPACED OUT

You know that the sun provides Earth with heat and light. You might also know that it's a giant ball of gas. But did you know that the sun contains 99.8% of our solar system's total mass? Here's some information about the other 0.2% that's orbiting around it.

Planets are the largest bodies that orbit the sun. There are nine: four small, rocky inner planets (Mercury, Venus, Earth, Mars); four large, gassy outer planets (Saturn, Jupiter, Neptune, Uranus); and Pluto—a wayward rock smaller than our moon.

Asteroids are solid chunks of rock or metal that can be as small as a grain of sand or as big as a small moon. Astronomers believe they are left over from the formation of our solar system. Millions of asteroids orbit the sun, mostly in the asteroid belt between Mars and Jupiter. Could an asteroid hit Earth? Yes. That's what some scientists think ended the age of dinosaurs.

Satellites are objects that orbit planets. Moons are natural satellites, and there are about 100 of them in the solar system. But there are also thousands of manmade satellites (most of them orbit Earth).

Comets are balls of ice and dust that orbit the sun in highly elliptical (oval-shaped) orbits. When a comet approaches the sun, it warms up and develops a gas tail that can grow to millions of miles long.

THE SINGING BALLOON TRICK

Can science be fun? Absolutely!
Amaze your friends with this trick.

HERE'S WHAT YOU NEED:

- Several large rubber balloons
- Coins of different sizes

HERE'S WHAT YOU DO:

- Put a coin in a balloon, blow it up, and tie the end in a knot.

- Hold the balloon in both hands, swirl it in a circle, and watch the coin spin on its edge inside the balloon.

- Now stop and listen. The balloon will hum while the coin continues to spin around in it.

- Notice that when you spin the balloon faster, the coin travels from the bottom to the center of the balloon. The higher up the coin goes, the higher pitched the sound: the balloon will "sing."

- Repeat these steps with another balloon and a different-size coin. If you get a bunch of friends together, you can create a balloon symphony.

...mystified astronomers labeled them "Little Green Men."

SO, WHAT'S GOING ON?

The inside wall of a balloon is super smooth, so once the coin starts rolling, it will keep going for a long time. Something else happens as the coin rolls faster inside the balloon. Each time it makes a full circle, the coin makes the balloon vibrate.

The number of times sound waves vibrate in one second is called *frequency*. And every balloon has its own unique *resonant frequency*—the point where the vibrations start to resonate and make a musical, humming sound. When the vibration of the rolling coin matches the frequency of the balloon, the balloon "sings."

* * *

BRIDGES HAVE RESONANT FREQUENCY, TOO

Soldiers are taught to march out of step when they cross a bridge just so they won't create vibrations that match the bridge's resonant frequency. Why? If they marched in step, the bridge could break apart.

Marching soldiers aren't the only danger. The Tacoma Narrows Bridge in Washington state used to sway from side to side under high winds, which is how it got its nickname, Galloping Gertie. But on one extremely blustery day in 1940, the winds caused vibrations that matched the resonant frequency of the bridge. And it continued for such a long time that the bridge collapsed.

THE BIG FLUSH

Don't let this bit of bathroom science scare you—Uncle John spends lots of time in there and he's just fine…almost.

IT'S A GUSHER!

When you flush the toilet, everything goes down the drain, right? Wrong. Minuscule water droplets containing more than 25,000 virus-carrying particles fly out of the toilet bowl and into the air. They hover for a few hours in your bathroom and then finally touch down on all surfaces near the toilet. That means they land on your soap, your washcloth, your towel, and even your toothbrush!

PUT A LID ON IT

You could put the top down before you flush…but it won't help. The next time you lift the lid, a lot of those virus-carrying water particles will still float up into the air.

So what can you do? Put a chlorine tablet in the toilet bowl (it will kill some of the germs) and keep your toothbrush in the medicine cabinet, not on top of the sink. And the next time you brush your teeth, run your toothbrush under hot water first. Don't spend too much time worrying about the gross germs in your toilet, though—there are far more dangerous germs on a kitchen sponge or cutting board…but that's another story.

The loudest insect is the African cicada—it's almost as loud as an airplane taking off.

DUMB CROOKS

More proof that crime doesn't pay.

THE CANDY MAN

An Arkansas man broke into a bank on a Sunday, only to discover that all the money was locked up tight in the vault. Rather than leave empty-handed, he grabbed a clock radio and a handful of candy. In addition to breaking-and-entering and burglary, this genius committed one other crime: littering. He ate the stolen candy all the way home and left a trail of empty wrappers on the ground along the way…that the police had no trouble following. What kind of candy did he steal? Dum Dums.

DIAL 1-800-DUMB

Two men from New York robbed a bank using their junk heap of a car for a getaway vehicle. They had spray-painted "FOR SALE" on the side of the junk heap—along with their phone number! Guess how long it took to nab them?

HOOK, LINE, AND SINKER

While waiting in court for his case to appear before the judge, a prisoner decided to escape. He bolted out of the New Liskeard, Ontario, courthouse with the court officer right behind him. He ran through the downtown, onto the town dock, and jumped into the lake.

According to a recent poll, Americans' favorite car colors are white and silver.

When the cops got to the end of the dock, there was the escaped prisoner, begging for help. He'd forgotten one important thing in his mad dash for freedom: he couldn't swim. The police saved him...and then arrested him. Again.

DUMB AND DUMBER

We saved the best for last. Two British teenagers decided to rob a store. Good idea: They wore masks to hide their identities. Bad idea: They forgot to cut eyeholes in the masks. First, they demanded money...from the wall. Then they bumped into each other and crashed into the counter. Finally, trying to figure out where they were, they pulled off their masks...right in front of a security camera.

Makes sense: One term for a group of giraffes is a *tower*.

I SCREAM, YOU SCREAM...

...we all scream for ice cream!

ICE AGES

Which is oldest—ice cream, sherbet, or snow cones? Snow cones. The Chinese were making desserts by mixing snow with juices and fruit pulps 3,000 years ago. Sherbet—or "milk ice"—came next. In the late 13th century, Marco Polo brought a recipe for fruit sherbet from China to Italy, but only a few people knew about it and the recipes became closely guarded secrets.

Historians estimate that sometime in the 16th century, some chef—no one knows who—increased the milk content in the recipe and eliminated the fruit...inventing ice cream in the process.

RICH DESSERT

Iced dessert remained an exclusive (and expensive) upper-class treat for a century. Then, in 1686, an Italian named Francesco Procopio dei Coltelli opened Paris's first coffeehouse, Café Procope—the first business ever to make ice cream available to the general public.

Other coffeehouses around Europe soon started serving it as well. By the mid-17th century, ice cream could be found in all of the continent's major cities...and by

---

Medical term for ice cream headache: *spheno pulatine ganglio neuralgia.*

the end of the century, people were virtually addicted to it. In 1794 Beethoven wrote from Vienna: "It is very warm here, as winter is mild, ice is rare. The Viennese are afraid that it will soon be impossible to have any ice cream."

ICE CREAM IN THE NEW WORLD

Ice cream arrived in America in the late 1600s, and became popular with many of the Founding Fathers, including George Washington (he ran up a $200 ice cream tab with one New York merchant in the summer of 1790) and Thomas Jefferson (he had his own 18-step recipe for ice cream and is believed to be the first president to serve it at a state dinner). First Lady Dolley Madison's ice cream parties helped make ice cream fashionable among the new republic's upper class.

CRANKING IT OUT

But ice cream was still a rare treat. Why? Because there were no freezers in the 1700s. Ice was very difficult—and expensive—to get.

Most ice cream was made using the "pot freezer" method: the ingredients sat in a pot that, in turn, sat in a larger pan of salt and ice. The whole thing had to be shaken up and down by one

What? HOWLER MONKEYS CAN BE HEARD CLEARLY UP TO 3 MILES AWAY.

person while another vigorously stirred it.

Over the next 50 years, two developments helped make ice cream America's favorite dessert:

1. In the early 1800s, "ice harvesting" of frozen northern rivers in winter months, combined with insulated icehouses that sprang up all over the country, made ice—and ice cream—cheap for the first time. By 1810 ice cream was being sold by street vendors in nearly every major city in the United States.

2. In 1846 a woman named Nancy Johnson created the world's first hand-cranked ice cream freezer. With this invention, ice cream was both affordable and easy to make for the first time. By 1850 it was so common that *Godey's Lady's Book* would comment: "A party without it would be like a breakfast without bread."

WE ALL SCREAM

By 1900 electricity and mechanical refrigeration had given rise to a huge ice cream industry. And it had become so much a part of American culture that immigrants arriving at New York's Ellis Island were served a "truly American dish" at every meal…ice cream.

*   *   *

FOUR BASKIN-ROBBINS FLAVOR FLOPS
Fig Newton
Brassicaseus Beer (root beer and horseradish)
Chile con Carne
Prune Whip

WORD ORIGINS

We found the origins of four COMPLETELY RANDOM words and present them to you in NO PARTICULAR ORDER.

SPONGE
Meaning: A porous skeleton inhabited by a group of tiny aquatic marine invertebrates

Origin: From the Latin *spongia* and the Greek *sphoggos*, meaning "water growth."

BOB
Meaning: Nickname of Robert

Origin: From an old Germanic word that means "shining with fame."

SQUARE
Meaning: A rectangular shape with four equal sides

Origin: From the Old French *esquarre*, which itself came from the Latin *exquadra*, which means "out of four."

PANTS
Meaning: Trousers

Origin: From a 16th-century Italian comic character known as Pantalone, who wore strange trousers. This gave us the word *pantaloon*, which first meant clown, and then the plural *pantaloons*, or trousers. The word was shortened to *pants* when it reached America.

COMING SOON

Inventions you might see in the next 10 minutes or the next 10 years.

DISPOSABLE CELL PHONE
Designed by a British inventor, it's a wafer-thin computer chip stuck on a piece of paper the size of a credit card. The phone, called P.S. Call Me, comes with a miniature earpiece and is good for only one call…then you throw it away.

DR. TOILET

Imagine a toilet that analyzes your pee and poop and then sends an e-mail to your doctor if it detects anything wrong. It also tells you if you need to add fiber to your diet. Not only that: it plays music, too!

NUTRITION PATCH

Don't like your veggies? Then don't eat them, absorb them! The military is working on a stick-on patch designed for extreme circumstances that will send vitamins and nutrients through the skin.

ELECTRONIC NEWSPAPER

Picture this: Your morning paper arrives on *e-paper*—a flexible "paper" that continually updates itself throughout the day. You download the news and read it, then roll it up and go. Or use it to download a book. Hooray, no more heavy backpacks!

ANIMALS TO THE RESCUE

Amazing tales of heroic beasts.

HIP HIP HOORAY

What mammals are responsible for the most human deaths on the continent of Africa? Believe it or not, hippos. But they're not all killers. Some of them are downright kindhearted—like the hippo a *Life* magazine photographer saw in Kruger National Park, South Africa.

A baby impala (a type of antelope) had gone to the river for a drink when a crocodile grabbed it. As the croc started to drag the impala under the water, a nearby hippo saw what was happening and charged. The crocodile was so frightened that he let go of the impala.

Suddenly free, the impala tried to run, but it was so injured that it collapsed on the edge of the river. The hippo pushed its lower jaw under the dying animal and gently lifted it to its feet, but the tiny impala collapsed again. The hippo put its lips to the little impala's wounds trying to stop the bleeding, but it did no good. As a final effort, the hippo tried to resuscitate the animal by opening its jaws and taking the impala's head into his own cavernous mouth, trying to breathe life into it, but it was too late. The hippo stayed with the little impala until it died.

WATCH THE BIRDIE!

When a sparrow crashed into a chimpanzee cage at the zoo in Basel, Switzerland, one of the chimps immediately scooped it up in its hand. A zookeeper who was watching expected to see the chimp eat the bird. But instead of eating it, the chimp just held the bird tenderly and studied it.

Other chimpanzees became curious and came over to see the bird. It was carefully passed from one chimp to another. Each chimpanzee examined the little creature, holding it gently in its hand, taking obvious care not to hurt it. Finally, one of the chimps brought the frightened bird to the front of the cage and carefully handed it to the very surprised zookeeper...who released it.

ELEPHANT BABYSITTERS

One afternoon, an African woman placed her baby in the shade of a tree while she worked. Soon after, an elephant herd strolled by and saw the baby. The elephants seemed to worry that the baby would be disturbed by flies, which can be a problem in that part of Africa. The mother watched, amazed, as several of the elephants pulled big leaves from the trees and covered the sleeping babe with them. The elephants were so gentle and quiet that they didn't even wake the baby. When the baby was covered, the elephants continued on their way.

Why do geese honk when they fly? One reason: To avoid midair collisions.

SPACE WASTE

*Here are some of the most disgusting facts
we could find about space travel.*

UFOS (Unidentified Flying Odors)
   • Some astronauts in the early 1960s had
   trouble with the plastic bags they used to
poop in. More than once, a wayward poop floated out
of the bag before the astronaut could seal it shut.

• Apollo astronauts left some boots and some bags of
urine on the moon to cut down on the weight of the
ship for the return trip to Earth.

• Since saving water is very important in space, there
was no laundry on Skylab. The astronauts were supplied
with more than 200 pairs of underpants. Dirty clothes
were thrown into a tank under the floor.

• Astronauts have to exercise daily to keep their muscles
in shape. So where does the sweat go when a person
works out in space? It doesn't drip off their faces or run
down their armpits—it collects in a puddle about the size
of a dinner plate on their backs. The astronaut has to
wipe it off quickly or the sweaty puddle will float away.

• Millions of people watched Buzz Aldrin of *Apollo 11*
take his first steps on the moon. But what none of them
realized was that the urine bag strapped to his left ankle
had broken, so he took his first steps with pee filling up
his boot.

Your armpit is also known as an *axilla*.

CHILD PRODIGIES

A child prodigy is a kid with extraordinary talents whose genius is recognized at an early age. (Uncle John was not a child prodigy...unless you consider farting a "talent.")

TIGER WOODS

Tiger Woods was born to golf. At only six months old, he was already imitating his dad's golf swing as he watched him chip balls into a net in the backyard. As soon as Tiger could walk, his dad put a golf club in his hand. (The club was sawed in half to be the right size.) In 1977, two-year-old Tiger was already so good at golf that he got to putt against the famous comedian, Bob Hope, during their TV appearance on *The Mike Douglas Show*. By the time Tiger started first grade, he was outplaying most adults. *Sports Illustrated* and other magazines wrote articles about this golfing wonder.

Total Concentration

Tiger's father, who was his coach and mentor, had him listen to motivational tapes designed to keep him focused only on the game. While Tiger played, his father would shout, wave his hands, and throw balls onto the green to try to distract him, but Tiger was able to stay focused.

Tiger won his first tournament when he was eight...and he never looked back. At the age of 21, he

---

Keep moooo-ving: Boston's street plan was based on existing cow paths.

became the youngest player ever to win professional golf's most prestigious competition, the Masters Tournament. In 2001 Tiger was the first golfer in history to be the reigning champion of all four major golfing championships at once: the PGA, the British Open, the U.S. Open, and the Masters. With his competitiveness, strength, concentration, and love for the game, who knows how far Tiger Woods will go!

BOBBY FISCHER

Born in 1943 in Chicago, Bobby Fischer was six years old when his sister taught him how to play chess. Bobby quickly became so thoroughly absorbed in the game that his mother worried. "Bobby isn't interested in anybody unless they play chess and there just aren't many children that like it," she said. She even placed an ad in the local newspaper—the *Brooklyn Eagle*—inviting other children of Bobby's age to come and play chess with him. But by then Bobby had already found the Brooklyn Chess Club.

Chess Master

By the time he was 10, Bobby was playing in tournaments and winning often. At 15, he became the youngest International Grandmaster in chess history. In 1972, at the age of 29, he became the only American

House pets? Plants grow better when you pet them.

ever to win the Chess World Championship. Then he disappeared from sight.

For nearly 20 years, chess fans wondered where he was. Many thought he was dead. Rumors spread that he had gone a little crazy and was hiding. In 1992 he reappeared to win a chess match in Yugoslavia and then disappeared again. Even today, chess fans are still searching for Bobby Fischer.

WOLFGANG AMADEUS MOZART

Mozart is perhaps the world's most famous child prodigy—and the most popular composer of classical music in history. Even today recordings of his music outsell those of any other composer.

Born in 1756 in Salzburg, Austria, Wolfgang could hear any sound and correctly identify the pitch when he was only two. There is a story that he heard a pig oink and yelled, "G-sharp!" Someone duplicated the pitch on the piano and it *was* G-sharp!

At age three, Wolfgang climbed onto the piano bench next to his older sister and started playing. He learned to play the piano in only 45 minutes! By the time he was four, he was making up his own compositions and playing the violin.

And at the age of six, he went on tour and played for all the kings and queens of Europe. He wore a velvet coat with lace ruffles and a small gold sword hanging at his side. Audiences adored him. Francis I of Vienna called him *"ein klein hexenmeister"* ("a little master wizard").

All-American sport? Costa Rica produces every baseball used in the major leagues.

Child's Play

At only eight years old, Wolfgang wrote his first symphony; he wrote his first opera at 11. This amazing artist could hear an entire symphony played only once, and then write it out note for note. He could hear a piece of music, and not only replay it, he could play it backward—from the last note to the first!

Mozart died when he was only 35 years old. But in his short life, this Austrian composer wrote many masterpieces, including symphonies and operas such as *The Magic Flute* and *Don Giovanni*. In fact, if you played every one of Mozart's pieces in a row, it would take you 202 hours. That's more than eight days of round-the-clock listening!

*   *   *

TWO MORE AMAZING KIDS

• **Louis Braille** lost his eyesight in 1812 at the age of three. Improving on the experiments of others who created raised-letter alphabets for the blind, Louis was 15 years old when he invented his own version: a form of raised-dot lettering. What's it called? *Braille*, of course!

• **Lotte Frutiger** climbed Mt. Allalinhorn in 1927. The mountain—located in the Swiss Alps—is 13,289 feet high and covered with ice. Climbing it would be quite a feat for an adult...but she was only eight years old.

Are they house-trained? The Inuit tribe of Canada adopts bear, fox, and seal cubs as pets.

LA CUCARACHA

Have you ever gone to the kitchen for a midnight snack and flipped on the light, only to discover 10 zillion cockroaches running for cover? Those little hard-shelled guys are everywhere. Why? They're survivors.

DIE HARD
Cockroaches can live in practically all climates and temperatures. They can live for a month without food and a week without water. And they can hold their breath for 40 minutes. Here are some more amazing facts about these amazing creatures:

• **They're old.** Cockroaches have been around longer than almost every living creature on Earth. They were here even before the dinosaurs. They are one of the most adaptable creatures on Earth.

• **They'll eat anything.** Cockroaches are perfectly at home in your kitchen—they love your food. But if you don't have any food, they'll eat the grease off your stove, the paint from your wall, and the wiring in your TV. They'll eat soap. They'll eat paper. They'll even eat the sweat out of your sneakers. Yum!

• **They're sneaky.** Cockroaches can go practically anywhere. They can flatten themselves as thin as a piece of paper and slip through tiny cracks. They have an oily coating that helps to make them extra slippery.

• **They're big.** There are more than 3,500 kinds of

cockroaches in the world. They come in all shapes and
sizes. The Oriental cockroach is about an inch long
and is shiny black. The Australian giant burrowing
cockroach is about the size of an adult finger. But the
biggest cockroach of all is the giant hissing cockroach
from Madagascar. It's about four inches (10 cm) long.
(Yes, it really hisses!)

- **They can fly.**
Sorry, but it's true.
The brown-banded
cockroach is one kind
that flies. Another is
the Cuban cockroach
(it's green). Good news:
the giant hissing cock-
roach doesn't fly.

- **They outnumber us.**
Cockroaches mostly live in
caves or under logs, but
there are some that really like living with people.
They especially like big cities. And they love big families. Put two German cockroaches (a male and female)
together in your kitchen cupboard, and within a year
you'll have 50,000 cockroaches.

- **They don't have a brain!** A cockroach's entire nerv-
ous system is in its main body, which means it has very
little of what you would call a brain. That's why—are
you ready for this—a cockroach can *live for 10 days
without its head!*

MIRROR, ЯОЯЯIM

Uncle John loves to look at himself (we can't figure out why), so he decided to look into the origin of mirrors.

THE DAWN OF MIRRORS

Sometime, hundreds of thousands of years ago, some early human (let's call him Og) happened upon a pool of water. Og looked down into the pool and saw a face looking back at him. He was probably terrified at first, maybe even thought about running away…until it dawned on him that he was looking at himself! And people have been obsessed with their own reflections ever since.

Thousands of years would pass before people figured out how to make their own mirrors. The first ones were made in Turkey from polished volcanic glass. In ancient Egypt, mirrors were made of bronze and had elaborately carved handles of wood, ivory, or gold. The Greeks created a school for mirror makers. Students learned the art of polishing metal with sand without scratching its reflective surface. And in Rome, mirrors were made out of gold.

THROUGH THE LOOKING GLASS

So when were glass mirrors invented? In the 1300s, in Venice, Italy—home to the greatest glassblowers in the world. The artisans figured out a way to put a thin film of metal (a combination of tin and mercury) on the

---

If you had $10 billion and spent $1 every second, it would take you 317 years to go broke.

back of green glass and thus invented the modern-day mirror.

The Venetians refused to tell anyone else how they made the mirrors. And to make sure their secret was safe, the entire glass industry was moved to the secluded island of Murano. Any worker caught leaving the island or smuggling out mirror pieces was put to death. The glassblowers grew very rich because everyone in Europe wanted to own one of their beautiful mirrors.

THE SECRET IS OUT

Finally, King Louis XIV of France smuggled two workers off the island and paid them to give him the mirror-making technique. The Venetian glassmakers discovered the spies, but it was too late—the secret was out!

In 1835 a German chemist invented the modern process of making mirrors, using silver as a reflective backing instead of tin and mercury. With his silvering process, mirrors could be mass-produced. They were no longer just for the rich—everyone could own one.

THE HAUNTED TOMB

The Caribbean island of Barbados is known for its tropical climate, its sandy beaches—and its restless dead.

THE CHASE FAMILY CRYPT

Col. Thomas Chase and his family were wealthy English settlers living on Barbados in the early 1800s. They owned a large burial crypt in the graveyard of Christ Church. One of their relatives, Mrs. Thomasina Goddard, was the first to be placed in the crypt. The following year Thomas Chase's infant daughter, Mary, died and her casket was placed alongside Mrs. Goddard's. Then the vault was sealed shut.

Four years later, Dorcas Chase, Thomas Chase's teenage daughter, died. But when the family unsealed the vault, they discovered something peculiar: Mary Chase's tiny coffin had been moved to the opposite side of the crypt—and it was standing up on one end. Mrs. Goddard's casket hadn't moved. Assuming the crypt had been broken into by grave robbers, the family returned Mary's casket to its proper place, laid Dorcas's coffin next to it, and sealed the crypt even tighter than before.

A MOVING EXPERIENCE

Only 34 days later, Thomas Chase killed himself. And when the crypt was opened…all the coffins were still in place. The crypt was again tightly sealed and would not be reopened until 1816, when another child related to the Chase family died.

This time when the vault was unsealed, the hinges on the doors were so rusty, that it took two men to pry them open. But when the family peered into the dark vault, they saw that the caskets had been tossed about the crypt...all except for Thomasina Goddard's, which was left untouched.

The mourners were baffled: these coffins weighed more than 500 pounds each. The one built for Thomas Chase was extra heavy. It had taken eight men to carry it into the tomb. Yet this coffin appeared to have been hurled across the tomb as if it weighed nothing.

When the next family member died, crowds of people showed up at the funeral to see if the coffins had moved. They weren't disappointed: all of the coffins were out of place, each one standing on end against the walls of the crypt. All, that is, except Mrs. Goddard's.

FINAL MOVEMENT

Everyone on the island was talking about the haunted tomb, so the governor of Barbados decided to investigate. He checked the walls of the tomb to make sure there were no secret passages. Then he had workers spread sand over the floor, so the footprints of any intruders would be seen. Lastly, he had the door cemented shut. He even put his own personal seal in the cement. Even if someone opened the tomb and cemented it shut again, they wouldn't be able to copy his seal.

Nine months later, the governor opened the tomb. What did he find? The seal was still in place, the cement had not been touched, and no footprints were in the sand. But every single coffin—except Goddard's—had been tossed on end, as if a hurricane had passed through the place.

The governor decided to put an end to this ghostly business. He had all the coffins moved and the tomb left empty. It remains so to this day...*or does it?*

* * *

"DOC, YOU GOTTA HELP ME" JOKES

Patient: Doc, you gotta help me—I can never remember what I just said!
Doctor: When did you first notice this problem?
Patient: What problem?

Patient: Doc, you gotta help me—I think I'm a smoke detector!
Doctor: It's okay, don't be alarmed.

Patient: Doc, you gotta help me—I get a sharp pain in my right eye every time I drink hot chocolate!
Doctor: Try taking to spoon out of the cup.

Patient: Doc, you gotta help me—my hair keeps falling out. What can you give me to keep it in?
Doctor: How 'bout a shoe box?

MIND READER

Would you like to be a mind reader like Uncle John the Magnificent? All you need is a turban and a trusty assistant. (Okay, you can skip the turban, but you do need a helper.)

ACT I: The Introduction

Lights up

You: "Ladies and gentlemen, I, (*insert your name*) the Magnificent, have the amazing ability to read your minds. With the help of my able assistant, (*insert your friend's name*), I will demonstrate my incredible powers to everyone in this room."

Pause for dramatic effect, then slowly scan the room, pausing to stare directly into the eyes of one or two people.

You: "In just a few moments, I will leave this room and wait in a soundproof booth offstage. While I'm gone, you will select one single object in this room. When I return, I want you to use your collective brainpower to focus on that object and I, (*insert your name*) the Magnificent, will identify that object."

Your assistant chooses someone from the audience to escort you to another room. That person will be able to swear that you didn't hear a thing.

ACT II: The Setup

Your Assistant: "Ladies and gentlemen, would you now

please pick one item in this room. It can be a piece of furniture, a small item of any sort, or even a person."

Your assistant takes suggestions and the group agrees on an item. Now your assistant will ask another audience member to go bring you back into the room. Don't let your assistant get near you again, so the audience will trust that you aren't cheating.

ACT III: The Payoff

You: "Before we begin, does everyone agree that I have no way of knowing what item or person was selected by you, the audience? All right, then I, *(insert your name)* the Magnificent am ready to begin."

Put your hands to your temples and close your eyes.

You: "Everyone, please concentrate on your selection."

Your assistant now moves around the room, pointing to various items, and asking you questions.

Your Assistant: "Is this the item?"

You *(pausing for a moment to think)*: "No."

Your Assistant: "Is this the person?"

You *(pausing)*: "No."

Your Assistant: "How about this one?"

You *(quickly this time)*: "No."

Your Assistant: "Is *that* the object (or person)?"

You: "Yes! That's it!"

Wild applause from the audience. Lights out.

Garden rule of thumb: Plants with blue or purple flowers attract bees and butterflies...

HOW THE TRICK WORKS

In every question, the assistant must use the word
"this." As in, "Is *this* the object?" When your assistant
uses the word "that," then you know *that* is the object.
You can be even more tricky and come up with your
own system. But start with this one first. Your friends
will think you're Magnificent!

HAPPY NEW NIAN!

Did you know that Chinese New Year is traditionally celebrated by setting off fireworks? Here's an ancient Chinese myth that explains why.

Once there was a terrible monster that appeared around the time of the new year. This monster's name was *Nian*, which means "year" in Chinese. Nian was very fierce—he threatened to destroy every last person. The emperor of China, fed up with his people being terrorized by the monster, asked the help of a wise man.

The wise man challenged Nian. He chided the monster for wasting his strength and ferocity on insignificant humans, who could never be a match for him. He suggested that Nian prove his real power by destroying other *monsters*. Intrigued by the challenge, Nian destroyed all of the monsters on Earth within a year, but then he returned at the start of the new year to terrorize mankind again.

Only this time, some children playing with firecrackers noticed that the fierce and terrible monster was afraid of the noise—it scared him away. The children told everyone about this and from then on, on New Year's Eve, firecrackers, drums, and gongs were used to scare away the last remaining monster on Earth—Nian.

AMAZING COINCIDENCES

More favorites from our "freaky" file.

CROSSED PATHS

The year was 1863. A Harvard student was on his way home to visit his parents when he accidentally fell in between two railroad cars at the station in Jersey City, New Jersey. Luckily, the student was rescued...by an actor. What's the coincidence? The student was Robert Lincoln, heading home to see his father, Abraham Lincoln. The actor was Edwin Booth, whose brother, John Wilkes Booth, would assassinate President Lincoln two years later.

WHAT'S IN A NAME?

In 1664, 1785, and 1820, three large ships sank at sea. Each time, only one man survived. Three different shipwrecks. Three different survivors. But they all had one thing in common: they were all named Hugh Williams.

TAXI!

In 1974 a man in Bermuda was riding his moped when he was accidentally killed by a taxi. Exactly one year later, his brother was killed while riding the same moped, on the same street, by the same taxi driver... carrying the *same passenger.*

TIME RUNS OUT

When King Louis XIV of France died, so did his royal clock. They both stopped ticking at the same moment—7:45 a.m. on September 1, 1715. Neither has run since.

LOOK OUT BELOW!

Joseph Figlock was walking down the street one day in Detroit, when a baby fell out a window and landed on him. A year later, the same baby fell out of the same window and landed on Joseph again. Luckily, neither of them was seriously hurt—either time.

OH, BROTHER

In March 2002, identical twin brothers, age 71, were killed in Finland in identical bicycle accidents along the same road—two hours apart.

LUCKY NUMBER 7

Anthony S. Clancy of Dublin, Ireland, was born on July 7, 1907. It was the 7th day of the week on the 7th day of the 7th month of the 7th year of the century. Not only that, he was the 7th child of 7 brothers. On his 27th birthday he bet 7 shillings on the 7th horse in the 7th race. The odds of winning were 7 to 1. The horse, 7th Heaven, did not win. It finished—you guessed it—7th!

*   *   *

"Shoot for the moon. Even if you miss it you will land among the stars."

—Les Brown

SIM MAN

If Uncle John were to create a simulated house, there'd be a bathroom in every room—even in the closets. And, of course, every bathroom would have a bookshelf.

DIGITAL REALITY

What's the bestselling computer game of all time? Is it a wild car-chase game? An auto theft game? A bullet-ridden blood-and-guts game? Guess again—it's *The Sims*, where players build a home, create a family, and design a neighborhood.

Players control the digital people and get them to do exciting things like take out the garbage, go to work, or make new friends. They marry other *Sim* people and even have *Sim* babies. The goal: To **simulate** life and build a healthy, sane world.

MEET MR. WRIGHT

And who came up with this brilliant idea? A guy named Will Wright. Wright has been creating simulations ever since he was a kid. He started out playing with model ships and airplanes and then got into computers so he could build robots.

The first computer game Wright designed was a helicopter action game called *Raid on Bungeling Bay*. That was in 1984. He discovered he had more fun building the levels for *Bungeling Bay* than flying the helicopters. That gave him the idea for *SimCity*, his first *Sim* game.

SIM UNIVERSE

He spent two years trying to sell the idea for *SimCity—The City Simulator*, without success. So Wright and a partner, Jeff Braun, formed their own company, *Maxis*, and built *SimCity* in 1989. It was so successful that Wright followed up with *SimEarth*, *SimAnt*, and *Sim-Copter*. *The Sims* appeared in 2000 and with all of its expansion packs has sold 18 million copies to date.

Now, with *Sims Online*, practically everyone can play it—and can play together. Your digital family can interact with other digital families online. Wright says, "There's a lot more of *SimCity* in this game than *Sims*. Instead of playing in a small neighborhood of about 10 houses, you're playing in a large city of around 30,000 and building an entire city—kind of a collaboration with everyone. You can form businesses or a household with other players."

HOW A GAME DESIGNER RELAXES

What does Will Wright do with his time? Besides working on more Sims creations, he surfs the fan sites every day and downloads cool things that Sim-maniacs have created. "It's really ironic," he says. "Now it's the fans out there who are entertaining us, the developers, with their creations."

Wright feels that playing games is not just for kids, it's for everyone. He rides around his office on an electric scooter, still builds robots and, along with his daughter, Cassidy, is a frequent competitor in TV's *BattleBots* tournaments.

SPACE JUNK

Can you imagine a steel bolt moving through space at 17,000 miles per hour? Compare that to an average bullet which travels through the air at only 2,045 mph. Well, up above our heads, thousands of high-speed objects are circling Earth at this very moment.

THINGS IN SPA-A-ACE

There are more than 9,000 objects orbiting Earth—all traveling at an incredibly high speed. Most of them fall under the category of "space junk"—stuff left over from space travel and satellites, such as old rocket parts, steel bolts, flecks of paint, and trash. And some of these items are *huge*.

So what's the problem? Manned spacecrafts and satellites could be damaged if they collide with any of the junk. Because of this very real danger, a government agency called the U.S. Space Command's Space Surveillance Center, in Colorado Springs, Colorado, devotes all of its time tracking objects that are orbiting Earth so it knows exactly where they are.

WHAT GOES UP...

There's another reason to monitor all of that orbiting trash: sooner or later it's going to come back down to Earth. In fact, a lot of it already has. So far, no one has been seriously injured by falling debris, but it's always a possibility.

The moon's orbit around Earth would fit easily inside the sun.

Here are a few of the objects that are whizzing over our heads at this very moment.

- **Satellites.** The oldest piece of debris still in orbit is the second U.S. satellite, the *Vanguard I*, launched in 1958. It worked for six years, then went out of commission. Now it just circles the Earth.

- **Booster rockets.** The upper stages of *Delta II* rockets—used to launch space vehicles and satellites—have been returning to Earth in large chunks since 1989. In Cape Town, South Africa, 700 pounds of white hot metal slammed to the ground around several farms in April 2000. In 1997 a 580-pound piece landed in Texas, just 50 yards from a house. A woman in Tulsa, Oklahoma, reported being hit by a small piece of charred metal. Put on your hard hat: there are nearly 50 *Delta II* rockets still orbiting Earth, waiting to come home.

High Mom: The first mother in space was Anna Fisher of the USA, November 8, 1984.

- **Trash.** What do astronauts do with their garbage? Sometimes they just toss it out the back door of the capsule, into space. Once it begins orbiting Earth, however, all of that rubbish adds up. During its first 10 years (1986–1996), the Mir Space Station released more than 200 objects—most of them were bags of trash.

- **World's fastest glove.** In 1965, during the first American space walk, *Gemini 4* astronaut Ed White lost a glove. The glove stayed in orbit for a month, traveling at a speed of 17,000 mph, and becoming the most dangerous garment in history. Luckily, it didn't hit anything and fell to Earth, burning up on re-entry.

- ***Skylab,* the first space station.** It's no longer up there, but when *Skylab* was abandoned in 1974, it became a ghost space station orbiting Earth. Then, in July 1979, it fell out of orbit. The people of the world held their breath, wondering when it was going to return to Earth and where it would hit. They hoped it would land in the ocean. But whole chunks of *Skylab* rocketed through the atmosphere and crash landed in western Australia. Luckily, no one was hurt.

- ***Mir,* the Russian space station.** It was abandoned after fifteen years in orbit. But Mir avoided becoming space junk when the Russians intentionally brought it crashing back to Earth on March 23, 2001. Like Skylab, Mir splashed down harmlessly in the south Pacific Ocean.

BIGWIGS

A bigwig is a "very important person." The term actually comes from the days when very important people wore really big wigs.

BAD HAIR DAYS

It's an age-old question: What do I do with my hair? Ancient Egyptians had an easy solution—they just shaved their heads and wore wigs. In ancient Rome women wore wigs, colored hairpieces, and braided additions to imitate the style of Greek statues.

Much later, in 1624, King Louis XIII of France went prematurely bald at 23 and hid it by wearing a wig. Thus began the "big hair" fashion for men. His son, Louis XIV, was also hair-challenged and continued the fashion. During his reign, 48 wigmakers worked night and day whipping up elaborate hairstyles for the king.

HIGH-PRICED HAIR

Wigs made hairdressing easy. Men and women didn't have to sit for hours having their hair styled—they just sent it out to a wigmaker. But wigs were expensive. One human-hair man's wig cost more than a coat, breeches (pants), shirt, stockings, shoes, and hat put together. So instead, people used alternative material, such as horse and goat hair.

By 1775 wig-wearing had reached its peak: the bigger the hair the better. Women wore wigs that were three

---

World traveler: The Danube River flows through eight European countries and four capitals.

feet tall. They even had birdcages, *with live birds*, built right into their hair. The fantastic hairdos had names like *The Butterfly* and *Sportsman in the Bush*. The hairdo *à la Belle Poulé* was a ship model in full sail resting on curls simulating the sea. To make room for these giant headdresses, carriages—especially in France—were built with openings in the roof just so women could fit inside them! And women whose carriages didn't have a hole in the roof had to ride with their heads sticking out of the window.

GRAND THEFT WIG

In London, wigs worn by barristers (lawyers) were so expensive that they were often stolen. Wig thieves wandered the streets carrying baskets on their backs. Hidden inside the baskets were small boys. At the right moment, the boy would pop out of the basket, grab the wig, and then disappear back into the basket. The thieves counted on the fact that the barristers would be embarrassed to be caught bareheaded and wouldn't want to call attention to themselves—or the robbery. Today, barristers and judges in England are the two remaining professionals who still wear wigs. The wigs are all made by hand from 100% horse hair...which may give those judges some horse sense.

National treasure: Today more than 700,000 Americans are over 100 years old.

DUH!

Some grown-ups say the dumbest things, don't they?

"The Internet is a great way to get on the net."
—**Senator Bob Dole**

"Smoking kills. If you're killed, you've lost a very important part of your life."
—**Brooke Shields**

"You guys line up alphabetically by height."
—**Bill Peterson, football coach**

"Outside of the killings, Washington has one of the lowest crime rates in the country."
—**Mayor Marion Barry, Washington, D.C.**

"I've worked it out: You can sleep a third of your life, so if you can reduce that to a quarter, you have more time awake."
—**Nicole Kidman**

"I was asked to come to Chicago because Chicago is one of our 52 states."
—**Raquel Welch, actress**

"Strangely, in slow-motion replay, the ball seemed to hang in the air for even longer."
—**David Acfield, newscaster**

"The doctors X-rayed my head and found nothing."
—**Dizzy Dean, baseball great**

"I get to go to lots of overseas places, like Canada."
—**Britney Spears**

"Things are more like they are now than they ever were before."
—**President Dwight D. Eisenhower**

KID INVENTORS

A great idea can come to a six-year-old as easily as it can come to someone who is 50. Here are four kids who had a bright idea, acted on it, and made history.

IT'S A GRAND OLD FLAG

Have you ever wondered if anyone really wins those "Send in your drawing" contests? Well, they do. In 1926, 13-year-old Bennie Benson entered a flag-designing contest for the territory of Alaska. This Native American boy chose blue for his background, representing the Alaskan sky and the state flower, the forget-me-not. In the foreground, he drew the Big Dipper, symbolizing strength, and the North Star, representing Alaska's northern location.

Bennie won the contest—he received a $1,000 scholarship and a watch. Thirty-three years later, in 1959, Alaska became a state...and Bennie's flag became the official state flag.

MAKIN BACON

One Saturday morning, when Abigail Fleck was eight years old, her dad was cooking bacon in the microwave. Usually, he used paper towels to soak up the grease, but that morning he couldn't find any. So he reached for the newspaper, which really upset her mom. When Abigail's dad said, "I guess I could just stand here and let it drip dry," Abigail got her great idea.

Why couldn't the bacon hang on something, sort of like a clothesline, while it cooked? Then the grease could drip into a bowl below it. They wouldn't need paper towels, or newspaper, or anything. Brilliant!

Abigail and her dad went to work and invented Makin Bacon. It's a microwave-safe plastic dish that has three T-shaped supports in the middle. Now, people all over America are using this simple device and... makin' bacon!

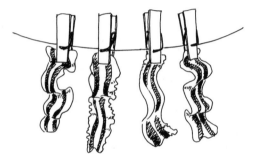

PACEMATE AND KIDKARE

What's more incredible than one award-winning young inventor? How about two award-winning inventors... who are brothers! And they didn't even work on the same invention. Brandon and Spencer Whale each had their own bright ideas. They both won awards in the Student Ideas for a Better America contest for their inventions, and they're the youngest kids ever to be voted into the National Gallery for Young Inventors.

Brandon's Idea: PaceMate. Brandon's mom had a heart problem, so she had a pacemaker put in her heart. After leaving the hospital, she had to send an *electrocardio-*

gram—which reported the strength and rhythm of her heartbeat—from her home to the hospital over the telephone line, using a modem.

But her wrists were tiny, and the electrocardiogram sensor bracelets were very big. Because of this, she had to have Brandon press the electrode on the bracelet against her wrist.

Brandon, who was only eight years old, had recently learned that an *electrolyte* solution—a liquid that's high in salt—was good for conducting electricity. He got the idea to soak small pieces of sponge in an electrolyte solution and place them between his mom's wrist and the electrode on her bracelet. He also added elastic to the bracelet to make the it fit better. Brandon called this new invention the PaceMate.

Spencer's Idea: KidKare. Spencer was barely six when he got his idea. Because Spencer and Brandon spent so much time visiting their mom in the hospital, they often went into the children's ward to play.

Most of the kids in the children's ward were very sick. They had to be given their medicine through an IV (intravenous) drip. (An IV is a little tube that is connected to a vein in your arm. It lets medicine drip into your body at a slow, even rate.)

The IV tubes were hung on metal stands with wheels so they could be moved around. If the kids wanted to move around and play, they had to lug the big heavy IV stand around with them. And if they wanted to ride in one of the play cars, a parent or

...American family would soon use personal helicopters for transportation.

nurse had to follow after them with the stand.

Spencer watched as adults tripped over tubes when they struggled to keep up with the kids in the play cars. Then it hit him: Wouldn't it be great if the IV stand could ride on the back of the cars? Then, parents wouldn't have to hold the IV stands or chase after their kids. Spencer designed a colorful play car that would carry an IV; he called it KidKare.

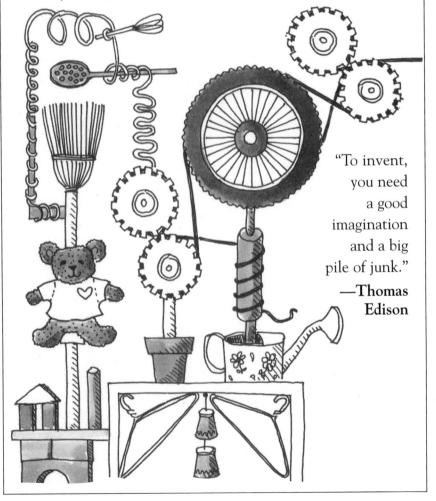

"To invent, you need a good imagination and a big pile of junk."
—**Thomas Edison**

Only girl ever to compete in a Golden Gloves boxing event: Amber Hunt (she was 12).

LEFTIES

Cosmic question: If the right side of the brain controls the left side of the body, are left-handed people the only ones in their right minds?

DID YOU KNOW?
- Only one person in 10 is left-handed.
- But if both parents are left-handed, the odds that their kids will be lefties increase from 10% to 50%.

- Boys are more likely to be left-handed than girls.

- Most gorillas are left-handed.

- The honeysuckle vine twines to the left (counter-clockwise), making it one of the few left-handed plants.

- The three main candidates in the 1992 U.S. presidential election were all left-handed: Bill Clinton, Ross Perot, and George H. W. Bush.

- At any given time, 40% of the top pro tennis players are lefties.

- Neil Armstrong, the first astronaut on the moon, took "One giant leap for mankind" with his left foot.

- It's against polo rules to play left-handed.

- Some primitive societies discriminated against left-handed people. They thought lefties were evil—and lefties often feared for their lives. Children caught using their left hand for reaching and grabbing were often scolded and forced to use their right hand in order to

---

Skateboarding or surfing with your left foot in back is called riding "goofy-foot."

make it dominant. Some parents even tied their child's left hand behind their back or down at their side, forcing them to use their right hand.

• In ancient Japan, a man could ask for a divorce if he discovered that his wife was left-handed.

• In 1890 the baseball diamond in Chicago was built to protect batters from the late-afternoon sun. That meant a pitcher would face west and normally throw with his right arm, which was on the north side. If he pitched with his left, he was a "southpaw," which is what left-handed pitchers (and other people) are still called today.

LEFT BEHIND

Let's face it, it's a right-handed world—most products and tools are made for righties. Some examples: scissors, school desks, manual pencil sharpeners, violins, saxophones, carrot peelers, can openers, power tools, wrist watches, and rifles are all hard for lefties to use because they're designed for righties.

FAMOUS LEFTIES

Julius Caesar	Pablo Picasso
Joan of Arc	Marilyn Monroe
Leonardo da Vinci	Jim Henson
Billy the Kid	Julia Roberts
Ben Franklin	Keanu Reeves
Albert Einstein	Jimi Hendrix
Helen Keller	Bart Simpson

Traditionally, Mongolian children learn to ride horses before they learn to walk.

IT'S IN THE CARDS

Do you like to play Go Fish?…Crazy Eights?…or (in the bathroom) Solitaire? Then maybe we can interest you in a couple of pages on the origin of playing cards.

SUITS ME FINE

The first playing cards are believed to have come from the Mamelukes, people who ruled Egypt from 1250 to 1517. Just like today's playing cards, the Mamelukes' deck had 52 cards and four suits, with three face cards and 10 numbered cards per suit. But instead of today's suits—clubs, diamonds, hearts, and spades—Mameluke decks had swords, polo sticks, cups, and coins.

WILD CARDS

In the 1300s, cardplaying was a huge craze in Europe— until it was banned. Why were playing cards banned? Because they were used for gambling, which was considered evil. Religious people called them "the Devil's prayer book."

Paris, France, was one of the first: it outlawed cardplaying in 1377. Other cities soon followed, and by the mid-1400s, anti-card sentiments reached a fever pitch. During one public demonstration in Nuremberg, Germany, more than 40,000 decks of cards were burned in a bonfire. But none of the attempts to eliminate cardplaying worked. In fact, cards are one of the only things from the 12th century that still exist almost unchanged to this day.

CARD FACTS

• The four modern suits—hearts, clubs, spades, and diamonds—originated in France around 1480.

• Until the 1600s, all playing cards were hand-painted.

• For 500 years playing cards were much larger than they are today—about the size of a page in this book

• Not all card decks use diamonds, hearts, spades, and clubs as suit symbols. Traditional German cards still use hearts, leaves, acorns, and bells; Swiss cards use roses, shields, acorns, and bells.

• The joker is the youngest card in the deck—and the only American card. It was added in the mid-19th century, when it was the highest card in an American game called Euchre.

• In a standard deck of cards, the king of hearts is the only king with no moustache.

• The word *ace* is derived from the Latin word *as*, which means "the smallest unit of coinage."

DECODING HARRY POTTER, PART II

Wizard-in-training Harry Potter learns a lot of magic spells at Hogwarts School. They may sound strange and mysterious, but the words actually come from Latin, the language of the ancient Romans.

The Spell: Accio! (the summoning charm)
Latin Translation: "To summon."

The Spell: Cruciatus! (One of the "unforgivable curses," it causes excruciating pain in the victim.)
Latin translation: "To torture."

The Spell: Diffindo! (a charm used to break something open)
Latin Translation: "To split or open."

The Spell: Expelliarmus! (the disarming spell)
Latin Translation: *Expello* means "to drive out." It is combined with *arma*, which means "weapon."

The Spell: Finite incantatem! (the spell that stops the effects of all currently operating spells)
Latin Translation: *Fino* means "end," and *incantare* means "to enchant."

The Spell: Imperio! (Another "unforgivable curse," it causes the victim to be completely under the wand-waver's command.)
Latin Translation: *Impero* means "to order, or command."

The Spell: Lumos! (the chant that causes a small beam of light to shine from the end of a wand)
Latin Translation: *Lumen* means "light."

THE NAME GAME

John means "God is gracious" in Hebrew. It is also a nickname for a toilet. Uncle John prefers the first definition… or does he?

POPULAR NAMES AND WHAT THEY MEAN

Girls	Boys
Emily (German) *Industrious*	**Jacob** (Hebrew) *Held by the heel*
Hannah (Hebrew) *Grace of God*	**Michael** (Hebrew) *He who is like God*
Madison (German) *Child of Matthew*	**Joshua** (Hebrew) *The Lord is salvation*
Samantha (Hebrew) *Listener*	**Matthew** (Hebrew) *Gift of God*
Ashley (English) *Ash tree meadow*	**Andrew** (Latin) *Manly*
Sarah (Hebrew) *Princess*	**Joseph** (Hebrew) *God shall increase*
Elizabeth (Hebrew) *God's promise*	**Nicholas** (Greek) *Victory of the people*
Kayla (Greek) *Pure*	**Anthony** (Latin) *Priceless*
Alexis (Greek) *Defender of mankind*	**Tyler** (English) *Maker of bricks or tiles*
Abigail (Hebrew) *Father's joy*	**Daniel** (Hebrew) *God judges*

Look at a blank piece of white paper after staring at a computer…

THE MICROWAVE

Microwave ovens are so common that it's easy to forget how rare they once were. In 1975, only 10% of homes had one. Today, more Americans own microwaves than dishwashers.

HOT DISCOVERY

Magnetrons, the tubes that produce microwaves, were invented by British scientists during World War II for radar systems.

These tubes might still be for strictly military use if it weren't for an engineer named Percy Spencer. One day in 1946, Spencer stepped in front of a magnetron with a chocolate bar in his pocket. Minutes later he went to eat the candy and found the chocolate had almost completely melted.

Spencer wasn't sure what had happened, but he wondered whether the magnetron was responsible. So he tried an experiment: He held a bag of popcorn kernels up to the tube. Seconds later, they popped.

The next day Spencer brought eggs and a tea kettle to work. He cut a hole in the side of the kettle, stuck an egg in, and put it next to the magnetron. The egg exploded.

MICROWAVES TO MARKET

Spencer shared his discovery with his bosses and suggested making magnetron-powered ovens. They agreed and patented the first "high-frequency dielectric heating apparatus" in 1947. It was five and a half feet tall,

...screen for several hours. What do you see? A lot of people see pink.

weighed more than 750 pounds, and cost $5,000—more than a house, so only railroads, ocean liners, and a few restaurants could afford them.

The price would remain high until the 1980s, when technical improvements made microwave ovens both affordable and practical for the first time. Result: today you can buy one for less than $100. Thank you, Percy Spencer!

*　　*　　*

FIREWORKS IN DECEMBER

In 1996 Chris Lee invited a few friends to his house for Christmas dinner. On the menu: a whopping 22-pound turkey…with stuffing.

Lee quickly stuffed the bird, put it into the oven, and then went into the living room to join his guests. A few minutes later, he checked his watch to see how much longer the turkey needed to cook. Uh-oh…no watch. Lee assumed he had left it at a friend's house. Wrong.

His watch was actually much closer than he thought: it was inside the turkey. While Lee was stuffing the bird, his watch had accidentally slipped off his wrist. And now it was roasting at 400°F. What happened? The watch battery exploded. The blast sent the turkey flying through the oven door. Pieces of oven, turkey, and what was left of the watch splattered all over Lee's kitchen. He spent the next four hours scraping the mess off the walls and ceiling. What did they end up doing for Christmas dinner? They ordered out for pizza.

When the *Titanic* sank, there was 7,500 pounds of ham on it.

ECRET-SAY ANGUAGES-LAY

Want to talk to your friends in a secret language? You could try to invent one of your own. But before you tackle that, try one of these. Ave-hay Un-fay!

PIG LATIN

Pig Latin, sometimes called Dog Latin, is the most popular secret language for kids. How popular? The Bible has been translated into Pig Latin. Online, Google even has a Pig Latin engine called *Ooglegay Earchsay Enginesay* (Google Search Engine). No one knows exactly how old it is (it's at least 100 years old) or exactly why it's called Pig Latin. What we do know is that it's easy and fun!

How Do I Speak it? Take off the first consonant sound of a word, add "ay" to it, and stick it on the end of whatever's left of the word. Words that start with a vowel just get an "ay" stuck on the end.

Samples:

you	ou-yay	party	arty-pay
me	e-may	cool	ool-cay
radio	adio-ray	movies	oovies-may

skateboard...ateboard-skay

Something to chew on: *Sitophobia* is the fear of food.

English: "Quick! Hide! Here comes my little brother!"
Pig Latin: "Ick-quay! Ide-hay! Ere-hay omes-cay y-may ittle-lay other-bray!"

OPPISH

This is an extra-secret language. It's not easy to master, but Oppish is definitely worth the effort. Oppish has been around probably as long as Pig Latin, and there are a few variations. We're only going to show you one here. Once you get up to speed, no one will be able to decipher your language. Unless they speak Oppish, too.

How do I speak it? Insert "op" after the first consonant of any syllable. For words that start with vowels, put the first "op" right in front of the vowel. ("Elephant" becomes "op-elopephopant.") In this version, it's not necessary to put an "op" at the end of the word.

Samples:

you	yop-ou	party	pop-ar-top-y
me	mop-e	cool	cop-ool
radio	rop-a-dop-io	hot dog	hop-ot dop-og

skateboard...skop-a-top-e-bop-oard

English: "Quick! Hide! Here comes my little brother."
Oppish: "Quop-ick! Hop-ide! Hop-ere cop-omes mop-eye lop-it-top-le brop-o-thop-er!"

UBBI DUBBI

The secret language Ubbi Dubbi was created for the

PBS television show *Zoom*. The code is simple to learn and, if you speak it really fast, impossible for a non-ubbi dubbi-ist to understand.

How do I speak it? All you have to do is add "ub" before every vowel sound.

Samples:

you	yub-ou	party	pub-ar-tub-y
me	mub-e	cool	cub-ool
radio	rub-a-dub-i-ub-o	burger	buburg-gub-er
	skateboard ...skub-ate-bub-oard		

English: "Quick! Hide! Here comes my little brother."
Ubbi Dubbi: "Quub-ick! Hub-ide! Hub-ere cub-omes mub-y lub-it-tuble brub-o-thub-er."

Want more? Check out our RESOURCE GUIDE on page 284, where you'll find websites that will help you translate words into sop-e-crop-et lop-an-gop-uages.

*   *   *

MORE SECRET LANGUAGES

There are actually dozens of secret languages already invented. Here are a few:

Bush Talk	Jeriqoza
Double Dutch	Gree
Cazarny	Fufa
Skimono Jive	Eggy-Peggy

...1) addlebrain! 2) dunderhead! 3) chucklehead!

MYSTERY EATS

Ever seen something weird on a menu and wondered what it was? Here are a few dishes that have puzzled kids for years.

Grits. Grits are small broken grains of corn, first eaten by Native Americans centuries ago. They are cooked in water and usually served with eggs at breakfast. They may look like gritty mush, but try them with butter or maple syrup. You may be surprised.

Tapioca pudding. Tapioca is a starch that comes from the South American *cassava*, or *yuca* plant. Cassava is dangerous because it has poisonous roots. But the Mayans figured out how to extract the poison (cyanide!) for their blow darts and turn the rest into tapioca. Other uses: tapioca flour can thicken soups and sweeten baked goods.

Sweetbreads. If you're looking for a cinnamon bread or a roll, don't order this. Sweetbreads are the *thymus* (throat gland) of veal (baby cows). They're considered a delicacy and are rich in minerals and vitamins. They're usually served creamed, curried, or covered with sauce. Why? Probably to disguise the fact that they're throat glands.

Chicken-fried steak. Is it chicken or is it steak? It's steak—fried like chicken. It's a favorite dish in the South and at truck stops. Dip a steak in flour and egg, roll it in bread crumbs, and then fry it like chicken. Add gravy, mashed potatoes, and biscuits, and you have a delicious, hearty meal...not healthy, but delicious.

The dye used to stamp the grade on meat is edible—it's made from grape skins.

THE GREAT MOLASSES FLOOD

*Here's the story of one of the most unusual—
and messiest—disasters in U.S. history.*

PRETTY SWEET
Have you ever tasted molasses? Made from sugar
cane, it's the stuff they use to make brown sugar
brown. It's also an ingredient in baked beans, candy,
and even animal feed. And when mixed with water and
allowed to ferment, it becomes an alcoholic beverage
called rum. In its pure form, molasses is a very sweet,
very dark, and very thick liquid—not as thick as peanut
butter, but a lot thicker than honey. And it's very, very
sticky.

In 1919 the United States Industrial Alcohol Company kept an enormous molasses storage tank in downtown Boston, near the waterfront. The tank was large
enough to hold 2.5 million gallons, and on the morning
of January 15, 1919, the tank was full.

STICKY SITUATION

What started out as a normal day in Boston turned into
disaster shortly after noon. People heard a low rumbling
sound, followed by a huge crash—the sound of the huge
tank bursting open. In seconds all 2.5 million gallons of
that gooey molasses suddenly poured out onto the street.

If you've ever been knocked over by a wave at the beach, try to imagine what it would have been like if that wave had been 15 feet tall, made of something thick and sticky like honey or pancake syrup, and was coming toward you at 35 miles per hour. That's what it was like that afternoon in the neighborhood next to the tank: people heard the crash and looked up to see a huge wave of dark, sticky goo racing toward them, making what witnesses described as a "horrible, hissing, sucking sound" as it destroyed everything in its path.

GOO-TASTROPHY

When the tank burst, pieces of it went flying everywhere. One piece smashed into the towers supporting an elevated railway, causing a section of the track to fall to the street just as the wave of molasses was passing by. The train managed to stop before it fell into the goo, but many people on the ground weren't so lucky. They got caught in the wave and had to "swim" for their lives.

Next the wave slammed into a nearby warehouse, smashing through the windows and doors and filling the building with so much molasses that the floor collapsed under all the weight. Everything in the building—including the people working there—fell into the cellar. The molasses destroyed other buildings too, including several houses that were reduced to sticky splinters, and the local fire station, which the wave knocked on its side and pushed down the street toward the ocean. (Luckily, it got stuck on some wooden pilings before it hit the water.)

RESCUE!

The whole disaster only lasted a few minutes, but when it was over, several city blocks were left under two to three feet of molasses, and hundreds of people (and animals) were stuck in the mess like flies on flypaper. Firefighters saved more than 150 victims by laying ladders across the goo-soaked wreckage and crawling carefully to pluck them out, one by one. Considering the size of the wave and the amount of damage, it's a miracle that only 21 people were killed.

YOU THOUGHT *YOUR* ROOM WAS MESSY

The disaster was over, but the mess was just beginning. Removing a couple million gallons of molasses from downtown Boston wasn't easy: fireboats spent weeks blasting it with water, and when that didn't get rid of all the goo, workers covered the streets with sand.

Climb it in December: The Eiffel Tower gets nearly 7 inches taller in hot weather.

But it was too little, too late—the mess had traveled all over town. Cleanup workers got covered in the stuff and brought it home with them, as did the thousands of spectators who came down to the waterfront to see the mess for themselves. People got covered in the sticky muck and tracked it everywhere they went, smearing streets, sidewalks, public telephones, and even the seats on streetcars with a sticky, smelly brown layer of slime. Soon it seemed like *everything* in Boston was covered in the stuff, and it was decades before the smell of molasses finally went away.

MYSTERY SOLVED

So what caused the tank to break in the first place? The investigation dragged on for more than six years, and in that time three major theories were proposed: 1) the tank was sabotaged by someone with a bomb; 2) the unusually warm January day had caused the molasses to ferment, giving off gasses that built up under pressure and made the tank explode; and 3) the tank was poorly designed and not strong enough to hold that much molasses. In the end investigators decided that the bad design of the tank was to blame, and the owners had to shell out nearly $1 million to pay for all the damage that it had caused.

*   *   *

Q: Why is your nose in the middle of your face?
A: Because it's the scenter.

LOONEY TUNES

Here are some fun songs to drive your
parents nuts on long car rides.

"Greasy, Grimy Gopher Guts"
(sing to the tune of "The Old Grey Mare")

Great green globs of greasy, grimy gopher guts,
Mutilated monkey feet,
Chopped-up baby parakeet,
French-fried eyeballs rolling down the dirty street,
And I forgot my spoon.

Great big gobs of ooey, gooey gopher guts,
Oldy, moldy goober nuts,
Little, turdy birdie feet,
All wrapped up in marinated monkey meat,
And I forgot my spoon.

"My Body Lies Over the Ocean"
(sing to the tune of "My Bonnie Lies over the Ocean")

My body lies over the ocean,
My head's hanging over the rail,
I'm getting a sick new emotion,
Will someone please bring me a pail?

Come up, come up,
Come up my dinner. Come up. Come up.
Come up, come up,
Come up my dinner. Kerplop!

"On Top Of Spaghetti"
(sing to the tune of "On Top of Old Smokey")

On top of spaghetti,
All covered with cheese,
I lost my poor meatball,
When somebody sneezed.

It rolled off the table,
And onto the floor,
And then my poor meatball,
Rolled out of the door.

It rolled in the garden,
And under a bush,
And then my poor meatball,
Was nothing but mush.

The mush was as tasty,
As tasty could be,
And then the next summer,
It grew into a tree.

The tree was all covered,
All covered with moss,
And on it grew meatballs,
And tomato sauce.

So if you eat spaghetti,
All covered with cheese,
Hold on to your meatball,
Whenever you sneeze.

Anteaters are toothless.

ANIMAL TALES

Fun facts about strange animals from the southern hemisphere.

KANGAWHO?

The word *kangaroo* means "I don't know what you're saying" in the language of Australian aborigines. When Captain Cook landed there in 1770, he asked members of the Endeavor River tribe what that strange hopping animal was called. They replied, "*Kangaroo*." Now there are thousands of "I don't know what you're sayings" hopping around Australia.

THREE-EYED LIZARD

The tuatara lizard of New Zealand has three eyes: two in the center of its head and one on top. The tuatara's metabolism is so slow that it only has to breathe once an hour.

PARDON ME, MA'AM

Harry the giant Galapagos tortoise is one of the oldest living animals on Earth. He was born around 1830—30 years before Abraham Lincoln became president. A scientist named Charles Darwin took the tortoise from the Galapagos Islands off South America in 1835. Darwin named him Harry and took him to Australia to live in a zoo. One problem: Harry isn't a he. At last report *Harriet* was spending her days lazing around the zoo in Brisbane, Australia, begging visitors for a neck scratch.

The average human body contains 30,000,000,000,000 red blood cells.

THE WHITE HOUSE GANG

Almost all U.S. presidents have had children.
Many have even had an unusual pet, like Thomas
Jefferson's mockingbird or John Quincy Adams'
alligator. But America has never known a
first family quite like Teddy Roosevelt's.

PRESIDENTIAL PLAYGROUND

When Theodore Roosevelt became president in 1901, the White House literally became a zoo. Roosevelt had six children, and they had the complete run of the place. They slid down the grand staircase on the family's good silver trays. Visitors often saw them roller-skating in the East Room. Guards reported being pelted with snowballs. They frightened visiting dignitaries with a four-foot king snake and dropped water balloons on the heads of White House guards.

One of the kids' favorite stunts was to crawl through the space between ceilings and floors where no living being other than rats or bugs had been for years. They rode their bicycles up and down the halls, and every member of the family had a pair of wooden stilts. No stairs were too well carpeted for their climbing, no tree was too high to climb, no fountain too deep to take a dip in, and no piece of furniture too good to use for playing leapfrog.

Besides humans, kangaroos are the only mammals that move mainly on two legs.

NATIONAL ZOO

The Roosevelt kids loved animals. The Executive Mansion was filled to the brim with them—dogs, cats, squirrels, raccoons, rabbits, guinea pigs, a badger, a black bear, a rat, a parrot, and a green garter snake named Emily Spinach.

The children's favorite pet was a pony named Algonquin. They would often bring him to the second floor of the White House in the elevator. The little spotted pony could then wander freely from bedroom to bedroom, visiting the kids.

Roosevelt led his children—and anyone who happened to be visiting—on obstacle hikes, family picnics, and skinny-dips in the ice-cold waters of the Potomac River. He taught his boys to box and his girls to run.

ALICE'S WONDERLAND

Roosevelt's oldest daughter, Alice, was a teenager when the family took up residence at the White House. She was wilder than her younger brothers and sisters, smoking cigarettes and racing around the countryside in a Packard automobile. Alice was a real handful for her parents and became the talk of the nation. Her father said, "I can be president of the United States or I can control Alice. I cannot possibly do both."

When the White House Gang, as the kids were called, left the White House in 1909, President Roosevelt said, "I don't think any family has enjoyed the White House more than we have."

The real name of Toto the dog in *The Wizard of Oz* was Terry.

THE WAVE

It's as much fun to do as it is to watch. Here's the story.

CATCH IT!

You've probably seen a Wave—maybe you've even been part of one. But did you know that the Wave first became famous during the 1986 Soccer World Cup finals in Mexico? Some fans in the stands leaped to their feet with their arms up in the air and then sat back down. Then the group next to them did the same thing. Then the group next to *them* did it. If you were on the other side of the stadium looking across the field, or watching on television, you saw a beautifully rhythmic and synchronized movement rolling through the crowd which looked just like...a large ocean wave.

Pretty soon, crowds across the world were doing the Wave during major sporting events. The Mexican Wave, as it was first called, has even had a few moments in Hollywood—once when Kevin Costner, James Earl Jones, and Amy Madigan did it in the movie *Field of Dreams* and another when it swept through the fans watching a jousting event in *A Knight's Tale*.

MAKE YOUR OWN

Next time you're at a sporting event, see if you can get the people around you to start your own Wave. There's nothing like seeing a massive Wave go around an entire stadium that was started by...you!

Three odd jobs: denture waxer, oyster washer, and sap collector. (No college degree needed.)

COOKING WITH UNCLE JOHN

Want to gross out your friends? Then go to the kitchen and let's start cooking. This recipe looks totally disgusting…but it's completely edible.

BARF-O-RAMA

FAKE BARF
Ingredients:
- 1/2 cup applesauce
- one package unflavored gelatin
- powdered cocoa
- oatmeal
- raisin bran cereal

Recipe: Ask an adult to help you with this recipe. Put applesauce in a frying pan and warm on medium heat. While the applesauce is heating, stir in the packet of unflavored gelatin. Remove from heat and add 1 to 2 pinches of powdered cocoa; stir well. Pour a small amount of oatmeal into the palm of your hand and sprinkle it into the mixture. Don't stir it completely— you want to keep some of the chunks. Next, add about the same amount of raisin bran.

Your brain uses about as much energy (10 watts) as a bulb on a string of Christmas lights.

When you're satisfied with the chunk factor, remove the fake barf from the pan and spread it out on a plate in a classic barf shape. Allow it to cool and harden for several hours. After it has hardened, use a spatula to remove it from the plate.

Now go fake out your best friend: Place it on his front steps, then ring the doorbell. When he comes to the door, remember to clutch your stomach and moan.

*   *   *

AND SPEAKING OF VOMIT...

Twenty ways to say, "I think I'm going to _____!"

- throw up
- blow chunks
- puke
- barf
- upchuck
- zuke
- hurl
- heave
- ralph
- drive the white Buick
- hug the porcelain
- blow lunch
- negative chug
- generate eject
- have an out-of-stomach experience
- power burp
- vector-spew
- toss my cookies
- yak
- throw some doughnuts

Smallest dinosaur: *Compsognathus* ("pretty jaw") was about the size of a chicken.

THAT STINKS!

*We should all take time to stop and smell the roses.
But just make sure they're actually roses and not
one of these putrid-smelling flowers.*

CORPSE FLOWER

The corpse flower is the stinkiest, most disgusting-smelling flower in the world. And if that's not enough, it also:

• Grows from a tuber that can weigh more than 170 pounds (normal-size tuber: a potato).

• Can climb as high as 10 feet.

• Grows three or four feet in diameter—as big as an umbrella.

The flower grows in the Indonesian rainforest and can be detected from miles away. When it blooms, it heats up and its aroma quickly spreads through the jungle. The stench smells like a blend of rotting meat, dung, and burnt sugar. Flies and beetles, who love the smell, flock to the flower, which helps to pollinate it.

But it takes a lot of energy to produce a stench that attracts bugs from miles away, so the actual flower spends only three days in bloom. In fact, the effort is so exhausting that the corpse flower plant might bloom only two or three times during its entire 40-year lifespan.

SKUNK CABBAGE

When winter finally fades into spring, the skunk cabbage starts to peek up out of the frozen ground along the edges of wetlands and marshes. But even though it may be the first wildflower you see, *don't pick it*! Skunk cabbage smells like a giant stink bomb.

Like the corpse flower, skunk cabbage generates heat. In fact, it can generate enough heat to melt snow. Its skunky, rotten-eggy, old-farts kind of smell wafts across the marsh. Tricked by the stench (which suggests there's something dead and good to eat nearby), bugs flock to the skunk cabbage, where they are dusted with the flower's pollen. Once the bugs are covered in pollen, they go on about their business of looking for dead things to eat and unknowingly pollinate the rest of the marsh. Stupid bugs. Smart plants.

STINK BUGS

Stink bugs come in all colors—green, brown, black, and red—and can be found in Europe, Asia, Africa, North America, and South America. They have flat, shield-shaped bodies and feed on plant juices. What sets these guys apart from other bugs is their defense mechanism. If you try to squish one of them, their body emits a pungent, evil-smelling liquid. It smells like rotting almonds to some people and just plain stink-o-rama to others. But that doesn't prevent people in parts of Mexico, Africa, and India from *eating* them. Some people say stink bugs taste just like apples. A stink bug pie? Yum!

How many people have actually walked on the moon? Twelve.

LET THERE BE MORE LIGHTS

If you turn on your local weather forecast tonight, you probably won't hear about these mysterious weather-related lights...but they're out there.

ABOVE-THE-STORM LIGHTS

Most people have seen electric lights in the sky below the clouds—lightning. But there's a whole family of glows and flashes in the sky above the clouds, too. Meteorologists call these very weird light phenomena *sprites, elves,* and *blue jets.*

• **Sprites** are red plumes of light that shoot 20 miles above a storm.

• **Blue jets** are cone-shaped rays of blue light that discharge at 10 miles above the earth, extending far above the tops of clouds to 30 miles high.

• **Elves** are huge blue-and-white disks that come from the top of a thunderstorm. Some grow to be 250 miles in diameter and extend 60 miles into the air. And they can vanish in the blink of an eye.

BALL LIGHTNING

No one is completely sure what ball lightning is. What we do know is that the phenomenon usually occurs just after a lightning strike. A "ball" can be as small as a pea

---

A million dollars in $1 bills weighs a ton and placed end to end, would stretch about 100 miles.

or as big as a car. It can glow as bright as a 100-watt bulb, but only produces 30 watts of heat.

These balls of light float in the air and move through walls. They can last up to five minutes and vanish either silently or with a big bang. They can change colors right before your eyes. Ball lightning has even bounced around the cabins of high-flying jets, scaring the living daylights out of passengers.

SAINT ELMO'S FIRE

Saint Elmo's fire looks a lot like a neon light. It's a type of continuous electric spark called a *glow discharge*. Unlike ball lightning, which floats freely in the air, Saint Elmo's fire is always attached to a person or an object. It tends to occur toward the end of a thunderstorm, snowstorm, or dust storm, but it's not a form of lightning. It's actually *plasma*—high-temperature ionized gas.

The glow of Saint Elmo's fire is often seen on the top of a ship's mast when electrified clouds are overhead. The mast appears to be on fire but does not burn. Saint Elmo's fire has also been seen on airplanes, on the points of steeples, and even on the horns of cattle. If it should dance around your head someday, it will cause a funny tingling sensation in your body. But don't worry, you'll live—the amount of electricity in Saint Elmo's fire isn't quite enough to be dangerous.

GHOST DOG

*Are ghost stories real? Who knows? But they
sure are scary! In this one, we discover that not
all ghosts come in human form. Some of them
are short and furry and have wet noses.*

BOO-WOW

There is a story told about a ghost dog that
helped two young girls on the Isle of Wight (off
the coast of England). The beach where the two girls
lived was very flat. When the tide was out, it was a long
hike to the water. But when the tide came in, it rolled
in as fast as a racehorse. Many people died there—
drowned because they weren't paying attention to the
dangerous tides.

One day in 1935 two teenage girls on their way to
Sunday school stopped to watch an ocean liner pass by.
They stood on the beach, unaware that the tide was
already circling their ankles, when suddenly a little dog
appeared. It was completely black except for its paws
and one ear, which were white. He barked furiously at
them, ran toward land, and turned around, urging them
to follow him. As the little dog ran, one of the girls
noticed something strange: he didn't leave any footprints in the sand.

TIME TO RUN

Before they could even discuss it, the girls suddenly

Some stars, called *neutrons*, can spin up to 1,000 times *a second.*

realized they were surrounded by water. It was up to their knees and any second they would be pulled out to sea by the undertow. The girls struggled to get to shore as the dog continued to urge them on.

As the girls ran behind the dog, they noticed something else: the water should have been up to the dog's neck or even over his head. But it wasn't. In fact, the dog seemed to be running *on top* of the water!

As soon as they reached land, the dog vanished. Now this was very strange. How could the dog just disappear? They were sure they'd seen a ghost. When they told their friends this story, everyone laughed. Saved by a ghost dog? What a joke! But they stopped laughing when the girls told the story to their Sunday school teacher.

SPOOKY TWIST

The teacher listened carefully and then told his own tale. He said that 40 years earlier, there had been a tragedy on the beach. Three little girls and their dog had gone to play in the sand. They, too, did not notice when the tide came in. As the water circled them, they tried to run back to shore. But the water was too deep for the littlest girl, named Mary. So the older sister put Mary on her shoulders and tried to run for land. But she stumbled and Mary plunged into the deep water.

The little dog saw Mary fall and swam out to try to save her. He paddled as hard as he could and was finally able to catch hold of her dress. He pulled her toward the shore, but the current was too strong for both of them. Mary and the dog were dragged under and pulled out to sea.

Days later, when their two bodies were found cast upon the shore, the little dog still had Mary's dress clenched in his teeth and Mary's arms were wrapped around him.

You could hear a pin drop as the teacher described the little dog to the class. "He was completely black, except for his paws and one ear, which were white."

*　　*　　*

YOU CALL THAT FOOD?

The ancient Romans were fond of eating a particular kind of rodent, known as a *dormouse*. So fond, in fact, that the upper classes raised them like chickens. The little creatures (which resemble small squirrels) were kept in specially designed cages and were fed a variety of nuts to make them taste better. Yum!

NO-NOS IN SPACE

So you're going into space. Congratulations! But before you blast off, there are a few things you should no...er, we mean know.

NO RUNNING WATER. You can't just turn on the faucet and brush your teeth. Why? Water doesn't flow in a weightless environment—it just breaks up into tiny droplets and floats around. So you just have to swallow the toothpaste or wipe it away with a towel.

NO BUBBLES. Washing yourself isn't easy because soap bubbles, like water, would float all over the spacecraft. That means you're going to have to use a towel soaked with alcohol or soap. And if you plan on washing your hair, you'll have to use a special dry shampoo.

NO BREAD. Bread means crumbs—and those little tiny crumbs could float into someone's eye (or worse yet, into the spacecraft's components). So if you want to make a sandwich, you'll have to use a tortilla.

NO BURPS OR FARTS. Space food is designed to be easily digestible so astronauts won't pass gas. Why? Astronauts discovered that if they burped, quite often they vomited. Can you imagine barf floating around a space capsule? And of course, a fart in that small an area would be enough to get you voted off space island.

Song sung most often in the U.S.: "Happy Birthday."

TRICK OR TREAT

*Halloween is Uncle John's favorite holiday. Why? It's
the one day of the year he looks "normal!" Here's
how this spooky celebration got started.*

ANCIENT ORIGIN

The ancient Celts in the British Isles celebrated
their new year on November 1. Their New Year's
festival was called *Samhain* (pronounced sow-wen), which
means "summer's end." Early Christians adopted the festival in the seventh century A.D., making November 1 a
celebration of saints and martyrs—hence the name All
Saints' Day or All Hallows' Day. (*Hallow* comes from an
Old English word meaning "holy.") The night before All
Saints' Day was known as All Hallows' Even (evening)—
which was shortened to "Hallowe'en."

ANCIENT MYSTERY

*What's Halloween's connection to ghosts and costumes? No
one's sure, but historians offer these three possibilites.*

Theory #1: The Ghosts Are Hungry!

On All Hallows' Eve, evil spirits roamed the Earth in
wild celebration, ready to greet the arrival of "their season"—the cold dark winter. And just for fun, they liked
to frighten mortals. One way for scared humans to escape
the demons was to offer them food and sweets. Another
way was to dress up like spirits and roam around with
them…hopefully going unnoticed. "That is what the

ancient Celts did," explains Francis X. Weiser in *The Handbook of Christian Feasts and Customs*, "and it is in this very form that the custom has come to us."

Theory #2: It's Visiting Day!

The Druids, a Celtic priest class, believed that spirits freely roamed the Earth on the new year—November 1—when the veil between this world and "the other side" was at its thinnest. People dressed up as ghosts so they could better interact with real ghosts. They'd trick the evil spirits by offering up a feast and then leading them out of town.

Theory #3: Hey! Go Find Your Own Body!

On All Hallows' Eve, everyone who died the previous year would rise up to select a human body to inhabit until the next All Hallows' Eve, when they would finally pass into the afterlife. To fool these unwanted ghosts, people disguised themselves as demons and paraded loudly through the streets. The scarier and crazier they acted, the better…because what ghost in his right mind would want to inhabit the body of a crazy demon?

MODERN HALLOWEEN

Although historians debate its origins, they all agree that Halloween came to the United States in the mid to late 1840s. When Irish immigrants fled the potato famine to build a better life in America, they brought the October 31 celebrations with them. By then most of the beliefs in spirits roaming the Earth had gone away, but giving people an excuse to dress up and act silly—that's timeless!

THE CHAIR TRICK

Uncle John has seen major jocks be humiliated by this trick at parties, but girls love it. Give it a try—we dare you.

YOU'LL NEED:
1. A girl   2. A boy
3. A wall   4. A straight-back chair

WHAT YOU DO:

1. Take your shoes off.

2. Girl goes first. Start with your toes touching the wall and step back two exact toe-to-heel foot-lengths away.

3. Put the chair on the floor between you and the wall.

4. Without moving your feet, bend over and place your forehead against the wall.

5. Grasp the chair and raise it to your chest.

6. Now, try to stand up while holding the chair.

EXPECTED RESULT:

Girls should have no problem doing this; but boys usually can't do it. Why? Generally, a boy's feet are longer, which keeps him too far from the wall. His center of gravity is closer to the wall than his toes, so it's nearly impossible for him to straighten up. *Note:* If your feet are so small that you can't fit a chair in two foot-lengths, sorry—it won't work. (Try again next year.)

Asia is the biggest continent in the world. You could fit almost six Australias in it.

BERG-WATCHING

Icebergs are really big, really cold, really beautiful, really dangerous, and really important.

HOW BIG IS AN ICEBERG?

Picture an ice cube about the size of Connecticut. That's the size of B15, the iceberg that broke off Antarctica on March 17, 2000. At 183 miles long and 25 miles wide, this massive berg—nicknamed Godzilla—rose 120 feet above the ocean's surface and bottomed out at a depth of 9,000 feet below, and weighed in at around four *trillion* tons!

WHERE DO ICEBERGS COME FROM?

Snow is almost constantly falling on the ice sheets of Antarctica (southern hemisphere) and the glaciers of Greenland and Canada (northern hemisphere). All of this snow gets packed down under its own weight and slowly slides toward the sea. When the compacted snow reaches the water's edge—usually after thousands of years—it forms a huge ice "shelf." Then cracks develop from the combination of more ice sliding down behind it and ocean waves battering the front of it. When one of these cracks gets large enough, a huge chunk of ice breaks off into the sea. That's when it becomes an iceberg.

As soon as it hits the ocean, the iceberg starts to melt—bigger bergs have been known to last up to two years in colder waters. In the meantime, ocean currents

---

and wind can carry an iceberg thousands of miles. This can be especially hazardous in the North Atlantic, where icebergs frequently cross shipping lanes. That's what sank the *Titanic* in 1912.

HOW DO ICEBERGS FLOAT?

You'd think that something that weighs trillions of tons would immediately sink to the ocean floor—but ice doesn't. Most substances shrink when they cool, but when water turns into ice, it expands. For an object to float, it has to weigh less than the amount of water it displaces, so because ice is less dense than water, it floats. But not all of it—between 70% and 90% of it is under water. (Try it yourself: drop an ice cube in a glass of water and see how much of it is below the surface.)

WHY ARE ICEBERGS IMPORTANT?

Scientists use icebergs to measure global warming. As Earth's temperatures slowly rise, some environmentalists speculate that the glaciers will break apart faster, causing more icebergs to fill the seas, and causing sea levels to rise. If the levels rise high enough, you'll need a boat to travel through New York City.

Other scientists believe that the massive amounts of fresh water contained in icebergs could be used to quench thirst and irrigate farms around the world. The B15 iceberg, for example, could have supplied the entire United States with water for five years—if only we knew how to extract it. The problem is that towing a million- or billion-ton iceberg is *very* expensive. Some Middle

---

Picky, picky: A year is actually 365 days, 5 hours, 48 minutes, and 46 seconds long.

Eastern nations have considered transporting huge icebergs from Antarctica to the Persian Gulf, but most of the ice would melt before it reached its destination.

ICEBERG FACTS

• The process of glacial ice cracking and falling into the sea is called *calving*.

• Icebergs come in many shapes and sizes:

Brash ice are tiny icebergs. They can be as small as an ice cube or as big as a baseball.

Bergy bits are icebergs that are larger than baseballs and smaller than beach balls.

Growlers range from 3 feet to 10 feet. Why are they called growlers? Because sailors often hear a growling sound as they bob up and down in the water.

Bergs are the large icebergs, the largest of which are called **tabular bergs.** Found only in the Antarctic,

they're formed when huge plates of ice break off of the ice shelf; B15 was a tabular berg.

• Most of an iceberg is under the water, so when someone says, "It's only the tip of the iceberg," they mean there's a lot more to the story then what's being told.

FOODS THAT WENT TO WAR

*What do you feed hungry soldiers? It has to be filling,
packed with protein, not too heavy to carry in
their backpacks, and—hopefully—tasty.*

OH MAN, CANNED HAM

What comes in a can and looks like a pink brick of meat swimming in golden jelly? It's SPAM!

Invented by the Hormel Food Corporation in 1937, Spam (short for SPiced hAM) became popular during World War II. Why? It was cheap and portable and didn't need refrigeration—all of which made it an ideal food to send into battle with U.S. soldiers.

Enlisted men ate so much Spam during the war— more than 100 million pounds of it—that many of them swore they'd never touch the stuff again. But when the soldiers came home, sales of Spam in supermarkets shot up…and remain high today.

For those of you who think Spam is made from eyeballs, noses, and other unsavory pig parts—stop worrying. The canned delicacy is made from pork shoulder, ham, salt, sugar, and sodium nitrate.

AUSTRALIAN SUPER FOOD

Ever heard of Vegemite? It's as popular in Australia as

That sinking feeling: Crocodiles swallow stones to help them stay submerged under water.

peanut butter is in the United States. Except for being thick and pasty, it's nothing like peanut butter.

So, what is it? Vegemite is salty, dark brown yeast extract, seasoned with a bit of celery and onions. Sounds gross, but Aussies love it. During World War II, a jar of Vegemite was placed in every Australian soldier's mess kit. In fact, they ate so much of it that Australia almost ran out of Vegemite and had to ration it.

When the victorious troops returned, Vegemite was hailed as a "war hero." Even today it's a source of national pride (and protein). If you'd like to give Vegemite a try, here's a tip from the Aussies: *never* eat it right out of the jar. This power spread tastes best on bread with butter and lettuce. Now you're eatin' Australian, mate!

PLAIN OR PEANUT?

In 1938, during the Spanish Civil War, a man named Forrest Mars encountered some soldiers who were eating bits of chocolates coated with a hard sugar "shell." The soldiers explained that the sugar formed a protective seal that kept the chocolate from melting. This gave Mars an idea: He ran home to his kitchen and whipped up his own little sugar-covered chocolates. He packaged them in cardboard tubes and when World War II broke out, he sold them to the U.S. military as a snack that traveled well in any climate. After the war they became available to the public in little brown bags, appearing in "Plain" and "Peanut" varieties. Have you guessed what these candies are yet? M&Ms!

IT COULDN'T BE DONE

A poem by Edgar A. Guest

Somebody said that it couldn't be done
But he with a chuckle replied
That "maybe it couldn't," but he would be one
Who wouldn't say so till he tried.
So he buckled right in with the trace of a grin
On his face. If he worried he hid it.
He started to sing as he tackled the thing
That couldn't be done, and he did it!

Somebody scoffed: "Oh, you'll never do that;
At least no one ever has done it";
But he took off his coat and he took off his hat
And the first thing we knew he'd begun it.
With a lift of his chin and a bit of a grin,
Without any doubting or quiddit,
He started to sing as he tackled the thing
That couldn't be done, and he did it.

There are thousands to tell you it cannot be done,
There are thousands to prophesy failure,
There are thousands to point out to you, one by one,
The dangers that wait to assail you.
But just buckle in with a bit of a grin,
Just take off your coat and go to it;
Just start to sing as you tackle the thing
That "cannot be done," and you'll do it.

There are more than two million species of life on Earth.

RIDDLE ME THIS

What's black and white and read all over? A blushing zebra...
and this page of riddles! (Answers are on page 284.)

1. A mother has seven children. Half of them are boys. How is this possible?

2. If there are five rubber duckies on the counter and you take away two, how many rubber duckies do you have?

3. What's different about the letters on the top row?

$$A^{BCD}_{EF}{}^{G}_{HI}{}^{J}KLMN^{OPQRS}_{T}{}^{U}_{VWXYZ}$$

4. How many letters are there in the alphabet?

5. It has holes in its top and bottom, its left and right, and all through its middle. But it still holds water. What is it?

6. How can you throw a ball a short distance and have it stop and then come right back to you? (*Hint:* You can't bounce it off anything or tie it to a string.)

7. Where is the ocean the deepest?

8. What gets wetter and wetter the more it dries?

9. What turns everything around but doesn't move at all?

10. What is big and slimy, smells really bad, has bubbles on its head, 82 eyes, seven mouths, a green shirt, and sings the blues?

PLAY BALL!

You kick them; you throw them; you even trip over them on your way to the bathroom in the middle of the night. Here are some facts about balls.

TOSS UP

Centuries ago, balls were made from whatever materials that people had on hand—leather or linen and stuffed with reed, straw, corn husks, or even small pieces of metal. The ancient Mayans discovered how to turn the sap of several different plants into the spongy substance we now know as rubber. And they used it to make solid rubber balls.

But the strangest, most awful ball of all: throughout history, the *heads* of criminals and enemies were sometimes used as balls. Greeks, Romans, Anglo-Saxons, and many other cultures did it. It was the ultimate insult.

GOLF BALLS

The first golf balls were made of wood. Later they were made out of leather, stuffed with boiled chicken feathers. Today they're plastic molded around a rubber core.

Around 1848 golfers realized that balls flew farther at the end of the day than at the beginning of the day. Why? They were all scuffed up. That's when they started adding dimples to golf balls.

American golf balls made today have 336 dimples stamped into each little sphere. The number of dimples,

---

Hike! A form of football was played in China as early as 500 B.C.

plus their size and shape, can reduce wind resistance, give the ball more loft (height), and send the ball twice as far as a smooth ball.

BASEBALLS

Every Major League baseball is sewn by hand, held together with exactly 108 stitches. Here's how it's done:

A baseball has a small cork core, which gets wrapped first with thin rubber bands, then with 369 yards of yarn. The hand stitcher then dips the ball in glue, places the "pill" (the glue-dipped ball) into a frame, and stretches two cowhide covers over it. The covers are pulled together with pliers and tacked into place. Last, the stitcher sews the covers together, using 88 inches of red cotton thread. It takes an average of five minutes to sew a baseball. What's the life span of a ball in a professional game? About six pitches.

FOOTBALLS

The first footballs were round and were nearly impossible to throw, let alone catch. Over time they became more watermelon-shaped. Finally, the American football evolved into the perfect catching, throwing, kicking, and running ball with a very odd shape…and a very odd name: *prolate spheroid.*

In the early days, the football constantly leaked air, so the refs would stop play for 30 mintues several times each game while players took turns blowing up the ball. Today, each NFL team uses about 48 balls per game. Referees bring in a new ball for every kick and punt.

Softball was originally known as "kitten ball," "mush ball," and "diamond ball."

UFOS

Look! Up in the sky! It's a bird, it's a plane, it's...

FLYING SAUCERS!

In 1947 amateur pilot Kenneth Arnold was flying his private plane near Mt. Rainier, Washington, when he suddenly saw nine gleaming objects flying in formation. He opened his side window and then looked again to be sure they weren't a reflection or a mirage. Arnold had no idea what they were, but he was able to calculate their speed: 1,600 mph—nearly three times faster than any plane could fly.

When he landed to refuel in Pendleton, Oregon, he told a newspaper reporter for the *East Oregonian* what he'd seen. He described the objects as moving "like a saucer would if you skipped it across the water." He said they had a batlike shape, but the newspaper reported the objects as "saucer-like." No one knows what Arnold actually saw—real alien spacecraft, an optical illusion, or maybe some experimental secret weapons—but we do know that's how the term "flying saucers" was born.

FOO FIGHTERS!

During World War II, pilots reported seeing glowing balls of light flying beside their airplanes. These were called "foo fighters," a term based on the expression "where there's foo, there's fire" from *Smokey Stover*, an old comic strip. The U.S. pilots believed that foo fight-

---

The Dead Sea isn't a sea, it's a lake. But it *is* dead—it's so salty that no fish can live in it.

ers were secret German weapons or surveillance devices. Only after the war did they discover that German pilots had also seen the glowing lights, which they thought were secret weapons from the United States.

CLOSE ENCOUNTERS

In 1948 Dr. Allen Hynek, an astronomer from North-western University, worked with the Air Force to help investigate reported UFO sightings. To make his research easier, Dr. Hynek divided the sightings into four categories:

Close Encounters of the First Kind: When UFOs are seen at a distance, but no contact is made.

Close Encounters of the Second Kind: When UFOs leave behind evidence, such as burns on the ground. Or if the UFOs interact in any way with objects on Earth, such as causing car engines to suddenly die or lights to turn on and off.

Close Encounters of the Third Kind: When aliens from outer space are seen.

Close Encounters of the Fourth Kind: When aliens communicate with people on Earth. (This includes reports of people being abducted by aliens.)

MEN IN BLACK

They're not just in the movies. In 1953 Albert K. Bender, organizer of a small UFO research bureau, claimed to have been visited by three "men in black." They knew of Bender's organization and warned him to keep silent about anything having to do with UFOs. After they left, Bender was sick for three days.

Since Bender's encounter with these three mysterious men, reports of MIBs (as they are called by UFO-ologists) began to surface all over the country. Here's what would happen: when someone saw a UFO and tried to tell the world about it, three men dressed in black suits, driving a big black car, would show up at their door. They'd warn that person *not* to report their UFO encounter. The MIBs often claimed to represent some government agency and would briefly flash an official-looking ID. When the MIBs left, the witness would feel terribly ill. Soon, the person would be too frightened to talk about the UFO—or anything else— they had seen.

Some witnesses have described the MIBs as "Asian-looking" with "exceptionally long fingers" and "metallic" or "electronic" voices. They are usually wearing sunglasses to cover their eyes and driving mint-condition black cars, like Cadillacs, from the 1950s.

Could the men in black be government agents trying to keep witnesses from talking about flying saucers or aliens from other worlds? Or could they actually *be* aliens, sent to silence us earthlings? The truth is out there…somewhere.

Tree's a crowd: More than a third of the U.S. is covered in forest.

LEGO MASTER

This could be the coolest job ever: You sit around all day playing with Legos; your supply of the little plastic bricks is endless; and you get paid a lot. Your job title: "Master Builder."

WORKPLACE HEAVEN

Inside a 203-acre complex in Enfield, Connecticut, is one of the most unusual offices in the world: A singing Lego robot rolls across the floor. A Lego bald eagle plays a Lego banjo on a Lego shelf. Tiny green Lego gremlins peek out from under Lego plants. And lying around on the plush carpeting in the middle of it all is a dedicated team of Legomaniacs busily building their next masterpiece. Who are they? The Lego Master Builders.

STEPPING THE BRICK

Here are a few success stories for aspiring Legomaniacs.

• As a teenager in the 1980s, **Francie Berger** wrote the Lego company and asked if she could order two million standard red Lego bricks. They didn't take her seriously at first, but after she built a working farm out of Legos they brought her on as a designer. She became the very first Master Builder.

• **Bill Bodge** built a model of Teddy Roosevelt and took it to his job interview. They told him to take it apart and create Carmen Miranda, the Brazilian

---

singer/actress famous for wearing fruit on her head. He did it—and got the job.

• **Kurt Zimmerle** spent an entire summer building an exact replica of the Biltmore mansion in North Carolina. He even built billiard tables with sticks and balls. Lego was impressed, but before they would hire him, they wanted to make sure he knew how to "step the brick" (Lego lingo for making round objects out of square pieces). So Kurt built a perfectly round Lego snowman. He was hired.

• "The goal," says Master Builder **Steve Gealing**, "is to make creations look so real that people have to look twice and say 'Was that really made of Legos?'"

LEGOLAND

What else have the Lego Master Builders built? Here are a few examples:

• Scale versions of New York City, Washington, D.C., and the California coastline—all down to the tiniest details, such as cable cars traversing the hilly streets of San Francisco.

• A 6-foot-tall surfing hippopotamus

• A 15-foot-tall replica of Albert Einstein's head that welcomes guests to Lego Mindstorms, a workshop where you use computers to control Lego Technic models.

• A 3D replica of the Mona Lisa

• Life-size giraffes, zebras, lions, and elephants. (You can see them on the Safari Trek at Legoland in San

---

The Earth has an approximate mass of 12,976,000,000,000,000,000,000,000 pounds.

Diego).

- A 54-inch replica of the Aztec calendar.

Sound like something you'd like to do? Get in line. They get thousands of job requests a year. It's hard to get in—but not impossible. You just have to be good. Really good. (If you can make round objects out of rectangular pieces, you're well on your way.) But here's the good news: you don't need any special tools, just your hands, a great imagination…and lots of Legos.

LEGO LORE

- Lego was started in the 1930s by a poor Danish carpenter named Ole Kirk Kristiansen, who went door to door selling hand-carved wooden toys.

- "Lego" is a contraction of the Danish phrase *leg godt*, which means "play well."

- Lego manufactures 400,000 2x4 bricks every day.

- Legos come in 84 colors—18 are translucent.

- The smallest Lego piece is the golden coin in the *Knights' Kingdom* set.

- There are two Legoland theme parks: one in San Diego and one in Denmark. It took 30 million bricks to build the one in San Diego. And if you think that's impressive: the Legoland in Denmark has more than 50 million bricks.

- It would take about 40 billion Lego bricks laid end to end to get to the moon.

YOUNG AUTHORS

Do you dream of being an author when you grow up? Well, you don't have to wait—lots of kids have written books and had them published.

CHILD AUTHOR: Anne Frank

HER STORY: Although she was not published during her lifetime, Anne Frank is probably the best-known young author in the world. Anne was a 13-year-old Jewish girl whose family was forced to hide from the Nazis during World War II. She kept a daily diary of her experiences with her family as they hid in an attic in Amsterdam, Holland. Eventually the family was betrayed and taken away to concentration camps. Only Anne's father survived. When he returned to the attic where they had hidden for two years, he discovered his daughter's diary and had it published in 1947 under the title, *Anne Frank: The Diary of a Young Girl.*

Anne's spirit shines in the darkness of wartime as she writes,

> It's a wonder I haven't dropped all my ideals, because they're so absurd and impossible to carry out. Yet I keep them, because in spite of everything, I still believe that people are really good at heart.

The Diary of a Young Girl has been translated into 67 languages, has been made into several movies and a play, and is one of the most widely read books by teenagers all over the world.

What'd they do before that? Trains didn't have toilets until the 1850s.

CHILD AUTHOR: S. E. Hinton

HER STORY: Most people think S. E. Hinton is a man, because every Hinton novel is about troubled teenage boys. But Susan Eloise Hinton is actually a girl. Her first book, *The Outsiders*, is about the poor kids— "greasers"—clashing with the rich kids—"socs" (short for "socials")—on the streets of Tulsa, Oklahoma. It was published in 1967, when she was 17, and has since sold more than a million copies. Because she often writes from a boy's point of view, she uses her initials instead of her full name. She says, "I figured that most boys would look at the book and think, 'What can a girl know about stuff like that?'"

During her life, Hinton has written several books that have turned into hit movies: *The Outsiders*, *Rumble Fish*, *Tex*, and *That Was Then, This Is Now*. Speaking of Tulsa, where she's lived most of her life, she explains, "It's a pleasant place to live if you don't want to do anything."

CHILD AUTHOR: Gordon Korman

HIS STORY: Canadian-born Gordon wrote his first book, *This Can't Be Happening at Macdonald Hall*, in 1975, when he was 12 years old. He wrote it because his new English teacher—who was actually a track and field coach and had never taught language arts before—gave an unusual assignment: every kid in class had to write a novel. Gordon wrote his novel and, amazingly, got it published by Scholastic. (He dedicated it to his English teacher, Mr. Hamilton.) Next he wrote *Go Jump in the Pool*. By the time he graduated from high school, Gordon had written and published five books. Since then he has written more than 45 books for kids and teens. Korman says that 50% of what he writes is based on things that really happened and 50% is imaginary. The Disney Channel TV series *The Jersey* is based on his *NFL Monday Night Football Club* book series.

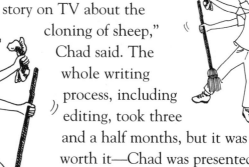

CHILD AUTHOR: Chad Merkley

HIS STORY: Merkley was a second grader in Snohomish, Washington, when he became the Grand Prize winner of Raintree Steck/Vaughn Publishers' 1998 Publish-a-Book contest. His book, *Too Many Me's*, is about an eight-year-old inventor named Albert who creates robots to perform his chores. The robots cause problems, so Albert decides to clone himself to finish all the work. The cloning idea turns out to be more of a problem than a solution. "I got the idea from watching a news story on TV about the cloning of sheep," Chad said. The whole writing process, including editing, took three and a half months, but it was worth it—Chad was presented with a publishing contract!

About half of the world's rainforests are in Brazil.

CHILD AUTHOR: Alexandra (Ally) Sheedy
HER STORY: Ally wrote *She Was Nice to Mice* in 1975 when she was 12 years old. It's the story of Esther Esther, an inquisitive mouse who is taken back in time through her family history to the days of Queen Elizabeth I and William Shakespeare. The book became an instant bestseller. But that wasn't Ally's first taste of fame—she had already been dancing with the American Ballet Theatre for six years. After her book was published, she was asked to write articles for the *Village Voice* and *New York Times*. As if being a dancer and writer wasn't enough, Ally soon added acting to her resume. By the time she was 15, she was acting in plays and in commercials. Then she starred in hit movies like *WarGames*, *The Breakfast Club*, and *St. Elmo's Fire*. Even though she had become a movie star, Sheedy never gave up her writing. In 1991 her book of poetry, *Yesterday I Saw the Sun*, was published to rave reviews.

If you'd like to try your hand at writing a book, check out the RESOURCE GUIDE on page 284 for a list of young author contests you can enter.

*   *   *

BRAIN FREEZE

When Ludwig van Beethoven was ready to write music, he would pour ice water over his head to "excite his brain." It also excited his neighbors—the water leaked through his floor and dripped into the apartment below his.

Chocolate, vanilla, corn, peanuts, potatoes, and turkey all originated in the Americas.

CHIRP! CHIRP!

Question: *It's a household pet. You keep it in a cage. And it sings. What is it?* Answer: *It's a cricket.*

J IMINY!
People in China and Japan have been raising an unsual kind of pet for more than 2,000 years—crickets. In Japan, people used to go to special clubs where they could sit and listen to the sound of crickets singing. Crickets in tiny bamboo cages were used as background music at garden parties. Some emperors in China had cages of ivory, jade, and gold for their crickets. And they even hired professional cricket caretakers.

VIOLIN CONCERTO

Only male crickets chirp. But how? They rub their wings together. The bottom of one wing has a sharp edge and is called the *scraper*. They rub it along the ridged edge, or the *file*, of the other wing and play it like a violin. Why do they do this? To attract females and to scare off other males.

PET PEEVES

Once they're comfortable, crickets will sing all day (and night) long. Is that a good thing? Well, it can get pretty loud in a bedroom. But if you decide to raise them, you'll need to keep them in a cool, shady spot. They don't eat much, just a piece of potato, apple, or lettuce every day.

Is it a secret? The dime is the only U.S. coin that doesn't say how many cents it is worth.

Bonus: If a stranger enters the house, your cricket will stop singing, which makes him a great watchdog. You can also tell what the temperature (Fahrenheit) is by the sound of your cricket. Just count the number of chirps during 15 seconds and add 40 to the number! (Or look at the thermometer.)

*　　*　　*

CRUNCHY CRITTERS

Uncle John found this disgusting (yet delightfully crunchy) recipe for all you cricket lovers.

Crispy Cricket Cookies

- 2-1/4 cup flour
- 1 12-oz. bag chocolate chips
- 1 tsp baking soda
- 1 tsp salt
- 1 cup butter
- 3/4 cup sugar
- 3/4 cup brown sugar
- 1 tsp. vanilla
- 3 egg whites
- 1/2 cup dry-roasted crickets
- 1 cup chopped nuts

Preheat oven to 375 F. In a small bowl, combine flour, baking soda, and salt. In another bowl combine butter, sugar, brown sugar, and vanilla; beat until creamy. Then beat in egg whites. Gradually add flour mixture and crickets. Mix well. Stir in chocolate chips and nuts. Drop rounded glops of dough onto an ungreased cookie sheet. Bake 8-10 minutes. Cool cookies and let the cricket-crunching begin. Enjoy your crunchy critters with a cold glass of milk. Bon appétit!

There have been 37 different animal shapes in Animal Crackers since their invention...

TOYS 'R' WEIRD

More strange tales of toys.

SEA MONKEYS

What are they? The magical, mystical Sea Monkey's scientific name is *Artemia nyos*. It's a close relative of the tiny brine shrimp and is a true freak of nature. This shrimp is born with one eye—but by the time it reaches adulthood, it grows two more. Three eyes! It also breathes through its feet.

Just Add Water

But the Sea Monkey is most famous for its seeming ability to come back from the dead. In 1957 an amateur naturalist named Harold von Braunhut noticed something weird about the tiny brine shrimp: It creates a protective cyst (kind of like an egg) that helps it survive without water. In this stage, it uses no energy and appears dead. When water is reintroduced, it springs back to life.

Three years later, von Braunhut began marketing little packets of brine shrimp eggs as Instant Life. He sold them through ads on the backs of comic books. Readers—mostly kids—would buy a package, add water, and *voilà*, Instant Life!

In 1962 Instant Life was renamed Sea Monkeys. Von Braunhut claimed their long tails made them look like monkeys (they don't). He also claimed they could per-

---

...in 1902. Current shapes include bears, gorillas, monkeys, seals, and giraffes.

form tricks and be trained to race each other (they can't). Still, there must be something appealing about them because people have been buying sea monkeys for more than 45 years.

PET ROCKS

One day in 1975, Gary Dahl was hanging out with his friends when the conversation turned to pets. Dahl didn't have a dog or a cat. He didn't have a bird or a fish either. According to him, real pets were too messy, too time-consuming, and too expensive. So, just for fun, he told his friends that he had a "pet rock." He said, "It's the perfect pet. Always behaves. Never makes a mess. And doesn't require food or water."

His friends loved the idea so much, Dahl was inspired. He spent the next two weeks writing a Pet Rock manual. Then he went to a building supply store and found the most uniform and inexpensive rock he could find—the Rosarita Beach stone from Baja, Mexico. (He paid a penny apiece.)

Dahl packaged his pet rocks with the manuals inside a cardboard box designed to look like a pet carrying case. Within six months, he had sold *three tons* of Rosarita Beach stone bundled in pet-carrying boxes for $3.95 each. More than five million pet rock owners "paper-trained" their rocks, taught them how to "roll over and play dead," and eventually faced the inevitable "pet burial"—in the backyard. And Gary Dahl? He laughed all the way to the bank.

Fill 'er up: Apples, avocados, melons, radishes, and raisins can all give you gas.

IF YOU WERE BORN IN THE YEAR OF...

According to Chinese legend, Buddha invited all the animals of the earth to a huge New Year's party. Only twelve showed up, so Buddha decided to honor them by awarding each one a year of its own. Chinese astrology uses these animals to tell us something about our personalities. What animal are you?

Rat (1936, 1948, 1960, 1972, 1984, 1996)
Think rats are nasty? Think again: they're a symbol of good luck and wealth in China and Japan. If you were born in the Year of the Rat, you are blessed with charm, wit, intelligence, and excellent taste. You love to flaunt your style wherever you go. But if you aren't careful, your devotion to your own self-interests might lead to greediness, boredom, and unhappiness. So think of others and you'll do just fine.

Ox (1937, 1949, 1961, 1973, 1985, 1997)

Oxen are natural leaders who never lose sight of their goals. If you were born in the Year of the Ox, you are loyal and honest—and possess the ability to achieve great things. The world may think you're stubborn, but your friends and family know you're really tender and affectionate. Your challenge: Learning to overcome your judgmental nature and allow others into your heart.

Tiger (1938, 1950, 1962, 1974, 1986, 1998)

Tigers are courageous and noble. If you were born in the Year of the Tiger, your sense of authority makes you a natural leader, and as such, you are demanding—but also charming…and fun. With a good cause to defend, you'll fight to the very end. Occasionally, you'll suffer mood swings and without focus, you tend to race aimlessly through life, but once you've found your center, you'll accomplish great things.

Rabbit (1939, 1951, 1963, 1975, 1987, 1999)

Rabbits are extremely attractive, sweet, and sensitive beings. If you were born in the Year of the Rabbit, you are very popular. You love to entertain, so your home will have the most comfortable and tasteful furnishings. Never one to fight, you will do everything you can to avoid conflict, even if it means looking like a pushover. By learning self-worth and assertiveness, the happy Rabbit will go far.

Dragon (1940, 1952, 1964, 1976, 1988, 2000)

If you were born in the Year of the Dragon, you are truly blessed—it's the luckiest and most powerful sign in the zodiac! You love being at the center of attention, and with good reason—you're a charismatic leader who loves to get the ball rolling and get everyone to play. But if you have to follow rules, you'll become miserable. You would do well to learn to balance your quest for success with flexibility, compassion, and tolerance.

Snake (1941, 1953, 1965, 1977, 1989, 2001)

Snakes are courteous, charming, diplomatic, and popular (which all applies to the BRI's own snake in the grass—Uncle John). If you were born in the Year of the Snake, you possess beauty and wisdom that is irresistible...and even a little bit dangerous. Highly intelligent and intuitive, you are often considered lucky in money. But it is really your willingness to work hard and your clever sense of perception that makes you successful. For you to feel more comfortable and less insecure, you must realize that confidence comes from within.

Horse (1942, 1954, 1966, 1978, 1990, 2002)

Always wanting to run free, the Horse is the wanderer of the Chinese Zodiac. If you were born in the Year of the Horse, you are energetic, love to travel, and are very good with money. Big bonus: you're a babe/dude magnet! You are also self-reliant and willing to do the work necessary to get ahead. But you're also impatient. Instead of waiting for things to happen, you'd rather get things done yourself. Once you learn to see the big picture, rather than just following whims, you will actually get a lot accomplished. So stay on course, you wandering Horse!

Sheep (1943, 1955, 1967, 1979, 1991, 2003)

Sheep are happy to spend the afternoon daydreaming. If you were born in the Year of the Sheep, then you are highly creative and spend a lot of time alone. You're not very well organized, preferring instead to be guided

---

Greenland is the world's largest island...but it has only 50 miles of paved road.

by your imagination. Your sensitive, timid tempera-
ment means that you often suffer bouts of insecurity
and worry. But with plenty of love, support, and
reassurance, you can learn to relax
and trust others. Then your
creativity can really shine!

Monkey (1944, 1956, 1968, 1980, 1992)

The happy-go-lucky Mon-
key is a party animal! If you
were born in the Year of the Monkey, you love to have
fun. You are also a good listener. You are intelligent,
knowledgeable about a wide range of topics, and even a
bit of a show-off... which sometimes gets you
into trouble. But having fun is what you're
all about, even if it means being a little
careless and accident-prone. Once you
loosen up and learn that the world doesn't
revolve around you, you won't be quite so
easily discouraged.

Rooster (1945, 1957, 1969, 1981, 1993)

Think of lawyers, brain surgeons, rocket scientists,
accountants—that's the Rooster! If you were born
in the Year of the Rooster, you are a quick thinker
who is practical and resourceful and possesses a keen
attention to detail. You're also honest and straightfor-
ward. But you tend to be a perfectionist—you expect
everyone else to have the same high standards as you

Bare fact: *Gymnastics* is from a Greek word meaning "to exercise naked."

and often dismiss those who fail to meet your expectations. Roosters need to live and let live—not everyone needs to be like them. Just remember: It's all good.

Dog (1946, 1958, 1970, 1982, 1994)

Dogs are generally considered "man's best friend," but in Chinese astrology, they are a little more complicated than that. True, those born in the Year of the Dog tend to be loyal, trustworthy, faithful, and honest, but only after their trust has been earned. If you were born in one of these years, you expect your friends and family to root for the underdog, you know the difference between right and wrong, and you fight injustice whenever possible! If you have a problem, just lighten up a bit. Relax. Don't worry, be happy.

Pig (1947, 1959, 1971, 1983, 1995)

If you were born in the Year of the Pig, you are a most generous and honorable person. You have a heart of gold and you're happiest when you're helping others. Highly intelligent and forever studying, you love to learn. You also love to take a nap or a bubble bath or just hang out with your friends. You are saddest when you don't feel needed. It would be good for you to open yourself up to all of life's experiences, even the ones that you can't fix.

John Quincy Adams was the first U.S. president to be photographed, in 1843.

FUTURE PERFECT

The world of tomorrow...brought to you today.

Today's Problem: You accidentally leave your lunch in your locker...for a month.

Tomorrow's Solution: The U.S. Army is now working on a peanut butter-and-jelly sandwich that lasts *three years*. It doesn't taste like cardboard, and will still stick to the roof of your mouth.

Today's Problem: You want to eavesdrop on your older brother, but the old cup-to-the-wall trick just isn't working.

Tomorrow's Solution: Simply slip on your invisibility cloak and walk into his room, totally unseen. An inventor named Ray Alden has applied for a patent for just such a device. Here's how it works: Using photodetectors and light emitters, clothing will map the surrounding area and change the fabric's coloration to match it—very much like a chameleon changes its coloring—making the wearer virtually invisible.

Today's Problem: You're going for a hike in the woods and want to take your computer along.

Tomorrow's Solution: Grab your miniature hard drive, roll up your computer screen, and then drop them both into your backpack. Roll it up? Toshiba has already invented a computer screen that rolls up like a piece of

---

Hot topic: Some scientists predict the global temperature will rise 37°F by the year 2100.

paper. When you want to use it, unroll it and plug it into your portable hard drive.

Today's Problem: Your family loves your house but not its location.

Tomorrow's Solution: Simply move it! A prototype of a "balloon cargo lifter" is already sitting in a giant hangar in Brand, Germany. This huge blimp is 20 stories high and is made of a high-tensile-strength fabric. It will be able to float a house from one location to another without worrying about roads, power lines, or traffic.

Today's Problem: You'd like to spend spring break on the Space Station, but there's no way to get there.

Tomorrow's Solution: A rope is dropped to Earth, you hop into the transport vehicle attached to it, and ride up like a yo-yo. How could a rope that long (200 miles) hold the weight? It's called BioSteel—made from spider silk, the strongest known natural fiber. BioSteel may soon be used for sutures, bulletproof vests, fishing lines, and really, really long rope.

Today's Problem: You've lost the stupid remote control…again!

Tomorrow's Solution: Lie back and relax. There's an amazing new remote control—a pillow with wire sensors embedded in the fabric. Embroidered on the pillow are graphics of numbers and volume controls. No more searching for disappearing remote controls, but look out for pillow fights!

We didn't invent this fact: On average, one U.S. patent is granted every minute.

DUMB CROOKS

And still more proof that crime doesn't pay.

COULDN'T BUY A CLUE

A man walked into a gas station with a knife and demanded that the attendant give him all the money in the cash register. The attendant replied that he had to buy something before she could open the register. The confused robber told her that he had no money, so he couldn't buy anything. The clever attendant told him that she was very sorry, but there was nothing she could do—she had to follow the rules. And the would-be crook left…empty-handed.

LOVESICK LOSER

While robbing a bank, the thief fell head-over-heels in love with the teller he was robbing. He got away, but he was so smitten that he actually called her, *at the bank*…to ask for a date! She talked to him—but not to make a date. She kept him on the line long enough for the police to trace the call.

HELLO, MY NAME IS…

In Long Beach, California, several employees of a large aerospace company got the bright idea to rob a bank on their lunch hour. They had it all planned out— except for one thing: They forgot to remove their I.D. tags while they were robbing the bank.

In 1992 St. Augustine, FL, passed a law requiring horses in the downtown area to wear diapers.

ANSWERS

BRAINTEASERS
(Answers from page 54)

1. Apples and oranges. Steve is an orange-eater. Why? The letter E appears twice in his name, as it does in the names Rebecca, George, and Helen.

2. Chop shop. The barber with the good haircut may seem like the obvious choice, but he's not. Since there are only two barbers in town, they would have to cut each other's hair. So the barber with the bad haircut is actually the better barber. The townspeople all know it, too, which is why they all go to the mop-head barber.

3. A fine find. Whoever made the coin would have had no idea that it was B.C. (before Christ). That symbol did not come into use until much later.

4. Dollars and sense. You have one $50 bill, one $5 bill, and four $2 bills.

5. Light Speed. It was daytime—the room wouldn't get dark for hours.

6. Soaked. One of them was bald.

7. A-quiz. Dead.

* * *

Never test the depth of a river with both feet.
—African proverb

How does he brush? A lobster's teeth are inside its stomach.

MASTERS OF DISGUISE
(Answer from page 99)

How Are the Masters Disguised?

Uncle John is the knight, *J. Porter Newman* is the gorilla, and *Mr. Tidball* is the Teletubby. How did Elbow Room figure it out? Here's how:

• He knew that Hairball's guess was wrong on all counts. Therefore, Tidball was *not* the knight, Uncle John was *not* the gorilla, and J. Porter Newman was *not* the Teletubby.

• Since the man in the gorilla suit whispered to Tidball, then Tidball wasn't the gorilla. If he was neither the knight nor the gorilla, he must have been the Teletubby.

• If Tidball was the Teletubby, Uncle John couldn't have been the Teletubby and since he wasn't the gorilla, he must have been the knight.

• Which left J. Porter Newman as the gorilla.

C-O-D-E BREAKERS
(Answer from page 151)

"I need help! Meet me at three o'clock near the throne room. Please be there and don't be late. A secret surprise will greet you. Bring the plunger!"

*　　*　　*

Q: What's a good thing to part with? **A:** A comb.

Research shows: Less than half of homemade dinners served in the U.S. include vegetables.

RIDDLE ME THIS
(Answers from page 256)

1. ALL of the children are boys, so half are boys…and so is the other half.

2. Did you say three? Nope—that's wrong. After you took two duckies, there were three left on the counter…but you have *two*.

3. The letters in the top line have curves; the letters in the bottom line all have straight lines.

4. Did you say 26? Wrong! There only 11 letters in "the alphabet."

5. A sponge.

6. Throw the ball straight up in the air.

7. On the bottom.

8. A towel.

9. A mirror.

10. Nothing.

*   *   *

THANK GOODNESS IT'S FRIDAY

One hundred years ago, the British government sought to debunk the widespread superstition among sailors that sailing on Friday was unlucky. A special ship was commissioned, named H.M.S. *Friday* (H.M.S. is a British abbreviation for "Her Majesty's Ship"). They laid her keel on a Friday, launched her on a Friday, selected the crew on a Friday, and put her in command of Captain Jim Friday. Finally, H.M.S. *Friday* embarked on her maiden voyage—on a Friday—and was never seen or heard from again.

RESOURCE GUIDE

Hey! We're not done yet! Now's your chance to take it beyond the pages by checking out some of these:

FOR YOUNG AUTHORS

- **Stone Soup**
A magazine written entirely by children.

    Gerry Mandel, Editor
    Stone Soup
    PO Box 83
    Santa Cruz, CA 95063
    www.stonesoup.com

- **Highlights for Children**
A kids magazine that holds an annual fiction contest.

    Fiction Contest
    Highlights for Children
    803 Church Street
    Honesdale, PA 18431
    www.highlights.com

Websites That Publish Young Writers

- TeenLit.com:
www.teenlit.com

- Dawn of Day:
www.dawnofday.com

- Kids on the Net:
kotn.ntu.ac.uk

- Katharsis:
www.katharsis.org

FOR SECRET LANGUAGES

- **Pig Latin translator:**
www.snowcrest.net/donnelly/piglatin.html

- **Oppish translator:**
www.davew.orcon.net.nz/oppish/oppish.html

- **Ubbi-Dubbi translator:**
pbskids.org/cgi-registry/zoom/ubbidubbi.cgi

FOR VOLUNTEERING

- **Kids Care Clubs**
975 Boston Post Road
Darien, CT 06820
(203) 656-8052
www.kidscare.org

- **Kids F.A.C.E.**
P.O. Box 158254
Nashville, TN 37215
(615) 331-7381
www.kidsface.org

- **Kids Can Free the Children**
Suite 300, 7368 Yonge St.
Thornhill, Ontario
L4J 8H9 Canada
(905) 760-9382
www.freethechildren.com

MORE WAYS TO VOLUNTEER

- **Youth Service America**
1101 15th Street NW,
Suite 200
Washington, DC 20005
(202) 296-2992
www.ysa.org

- **Earth Force**
1908 Mt. Vernon Ave.,
Second Floor
Alexandria, VA 22301
(703) 299-9400
www.earthforce.org

"There are millions of people in the world—but it just takes one to make a difference! Do something important—it has to start somewhere and with somebody. Start now! Be Somebody! Be One In A Million!"
—Melissa Poe, founder of Kids F.A.C.E.

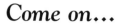

Come on...
TAKE THE PLUNGE!

To read a few sample chapters,
go to our website and visit
the "Throne Room," at
www.bathroomreader.com

Also available from the BRI:
An ever-growing assortment
of great gift ideas:

Tote Bags   Ball Caps

Mini Books   Toilet Paper

Mugs

Calendars   T-shirts

Bumper Stickers   ...and more!

THE LAST PAGE

FELLOW BATHROOM READERS:
Bathroom reading should never be taken loosely—we must sit firmly for what we believe in, even while the rest of the world is taking pot shots at us.

So sit Down and Be Counted! Join the Bathroom Readers' Institute. It's free! Send a self-addressed, stamped envelope to: BRI, P.O. Box 1117, Ashland, Oregon 97520. Or join us through our website at *www.bathroomreader.com*. You'll receive a free membership card, our BRI newsletter (sent out via e-mail), discounts when ordering directly through the BRI, and you'll earn a permanent spot on the BRI honor roll!

UNCLE JOHN'S NEXT
BATHROOM READER FOR KIDS ONLY
IS ALREADY IN THE WORKS!

Don't worry—there's more good reading on the way.

Is there a subject you'd like to see us write about in our next *Uncle John's Bathroom Reader For Kids Only*? Write to us or contact us through our website and let us know. We aim to please.

Well, we're out of space, and when you've got to go, you've got to go. Hope to hear from you soon. Meanwhile, remember:

Go with the Flow!